NOV 0 7 2014

DIS
Capital

sent you to me!

Author's Bio

At eight months old, the author, Karlene Robinson (Dr. Karlene A. Richardson), who was born in Kingston, Jamaica, West Indies, was sent to live with her grandparents. At 10 years old the author passed her common entrance to attend Camperdown High School. Despite the love she received from her grandparents and the bond she shared with her sister, Ilza, the author was destitute for a mother's love. This drove her to journey to the American Embassy, at only 13 years old to obtain a Visa to travel to the distant shores of America to find her mother's love.

The author attended Nassau Community College where she obtained an associate's degree in Liberal Arts and Science, a bachelor's and master's degree from St. Joseph's College of Maine, and a doctorate in health administration from University of Phoenix.

Today the author, a Pentecost, doctor in health administration and professor, lives with her husband, Gary, and two of her three children, Jevon and Jordan. The author's first born child, Taisha, lives with her husband Delano, and their daughter Sanaa.

Copyright © 2006 by Karlene Robinson
First Edition

All rights reserved. No part of this publication may be reproduced, distributed, or transmitted in any form or by any means, including photocopying, recording, or other electronic or mechanical methods, without the prior written permission of the publisher, except in the case of brief quotations embodied in critical reviews and certain other noncommercial uses permitted by copyright law. For permission requests, email the author, addressed "Attention: Permissions Coordinator," at the email address below.

Richardson Publishing Inc.
drkarlenerichardson@aol.com

ISBN-13: 978-0692228944

ISBN-10: 0692228942

Ordering Information:
Quantity sales. Special discounts are available on quantity purchases by corporations, associations, and others. For details, contact the publisher at the email address above.

Printed in the United States of America

There is no greater agony
than bearing an untold story inside you. . . .

~ Maya Angelou

Dare To Go
From Gutter to Glory

How did I make it out of the arms of the man who raped me? How did I survive the cold streets of Brooklyn and the unsecured door of the abandon building I called home? How did I make it off the corners of the streets hustling when so many others died, went to jail, or deported back home to Jamaica? How did I eventually become a doctor of health administration after battling the demons of feelings of abandonment by a mother, raped by a stranger, and abused by a spouse? How did I make it?

~~Karlene Robinson~~
Dr. Karlene A. Richardson

Characters

Karlei	Main character
Sulei	Daughter
Nathaniel	Son
Doug	ex-Husband
Mother	Mother
Chez	Younger Sister
Ilza	Older Sister
Sistermay	Grandmother / Mother
Daddy	Grandfather / Dad
Paul	Daughter's father
Jan	Sister-in-law/Doug's sister
Tiffany	Best Friend 1
Gary	Best Friend's (#1) husband
Dawn	Mother's friend's daughter
Peter	Father's cousin
Jamel	Sulei's friend's father
Steven	Best Friend 2

This is a true life story. The names of characters have been changed to protect the innocent, the guilty who is still not ready to admit their guilt and still claims their innocence, and the bystanders who wished not to have been a witness . . . . and then there is my story, their story, and the truth. You will read but not judge. You will understand yet not assume. At least, I hope so . . . thanks for choosing to share in this special journal entry of my life!

*This book is dedicated to my three children
Taisha, Jevon, and Jordan*

*My granddaughter, Sanaa and son-in-law
Delano*

*The completion of this book is credited to Gary
My Prayer Partner
Husband
Friend
Lover
Soul mate &
God's Gift to Me*

♥

So Yuhh Waan to Come to Fah'rin?

Fah'rin is not all that it is thought to be
Families are broken amidst controversies
It's a dog eat dog world
At least that's what they say
In this land of opportunity
All focus is on money

Don't believe the hype
Of the foreigners' lies
As they work their live-in jobs or sell drugs
Come back wearing name brands and nuff gold
Around their necks to let you think
Fah'rin is everything

It is a very tricky place
Today you're rich
Tomorrow homeless
Today many friends
Tomorrow enemies

So yuhh waan to come to Fah'rin?
T'ink yuhh can handle dis?

Hi,

   I came to this country without a green card in search of a mother's love. But instead, I found the cold streets of Brooklyn, New York. I struggled to survive. I had no money, no food, no clothes, no home. But I made it. I survived.

   In 1987 I was homeless, eating from the garbage. Today I am a doctor of health administration. I began my doctoral journey in December 2008 and completed January 2013. If I did it, you can too. All it takes is faith in God to know HE will see you through. Whatever you're going through, HE will give you the strength to make it to the end. God does not lead you to a place where HE will not bring you through.

   As you read my diary, be positive. Please do not judge, lest ye be judged. This is my version of my experience. There are several sides to any story . . . the author's, everyone else's, and God's. Ask for God to let you see the meaning, and not the blame. Each experience we go through is meant to give us strength. So I hope and pray that there is inspiration in the pages that follow. Pray for me as I pray for you and thanks for your support!

Love,
Your Sister in Christ

Dr. Karlene R.

Thanks . . .

Thanks to all who helped me along my way. Who offered a night's rest. Who offered me a plate of food. Who gave a quarter as I stood on the corners of Monroe Street and Nostrand Avenue in Brooklyn, New York, to earn enough money to buy milk for my daughter, or her pamper. Thanks to the man who allowed me to use his phone in his house on Fulton Street. Thanks to my daughter's godmother for allowing me to stay at her house during the time I was homeless.

Thanks to my mother who gave me life – the greatest gift of all. Thanks to my daughter – so small, yet strength so great. Thanks to my sons, whose hugs comforted. Thanks Tiffany, you showed me the way to a great church.

Pastor Dawson, Sister Dawson, Sis. Chin, Sis. Davis . . . how can I say thanks? Your support, your love . . . Thanks.

Thanks to Steven for being a friend.

Thanks to Chez, my younger sister, always listening. Ilza, you are my heart, thanks big sister. \My granddaddy and grandmother, I know you guide me still. And Mama . . . how can I not say thanks Mama? And to my uncle Ty, you started this! You gave me my first tuition. Thanks Uncle! Thanks to Auntie Martha for that experience at 13 years old, and for teaching me about life! Thanks Uncle Marshall, you led the way of this pilgrimage!

Thanks to all my students at ASA College for allowing me to teach *and* to learn. You were a part of my healing journey.

Thanks to the man in the restaurant on Church Avenue in Brooklyn, New York who was the cook, and gave me and my daughter dinner every night, and baked us a sweet potato pudding every night. Yet, you never asked me my name. You never entered my house. I gave you a gift of gold. If you ever read this book, please reach out to me. I need to formally say thanks. You never knew it but you kept us alive with your food. If you can remind me of the gift of gold I gave you, I know it's you, and will be thankful!

Thanks to Gary, the man who endured my absence at nights, yet gave me his presence and support till dawn came.

But most importantly thanks to God. Deliverer, Keeper, Comforter, Way-maker, Provider, and a whole lot more that it would take another book to list everything you are to me!

My Pastor, my Pastor . . . Pastor Clarence Gardener! I love you with all my heart Sir! Thank you for listening to the call of God! And for your patience as I try to find the meaning behind my existence and my purpose in life! I now know.

If I've not mentioned you, it's not deliberate.

Thanks and thanks again.

And just to note . . . to all the English majors who may read my book, sentence fragments were deliberate, and so were minor grammatical errors. Sometimes correcting these take away the very essence of the intent of a message.

Visit me at www.drkarlenerichardson.webs.com

PRELUDE

IN SEARCH OF...

Riding the Long Island Railroad to work, the first day of my new job, it was still hard to believe that here I was a college professor. Me. A college professor. Once again here I was heading to Brooklyn, but this time it was different. I wasn't homeless anymore. I wasn't alone in the big cold city of New York anymore, and I no longer lived on the 'A' train with my baby. I didn't need to beg for quarters on the streets anymore, and I did not have to depend on the food from the garbage put there by the men who worked on the abandoned home I called home.

I now had three children, a wonderful man in my life [God] and my wonderful and supportive husband. I still did not have the mansion or a Benz, but we bought a home and had vehicles to drive, so mmm . . . can't complain.

I had finished my Associates degree at Nassau Community College, my Bachelors and Masters at Saint Joseph's College of Maine, and recently completed my doctorate in health administration. I had fought society's statistics. But I must be honest – it wasn't easy.

As I exited the train and walked briskly on Flatbush Avenue towards Willoughby Street to where the community college was, where I was employed to teach,

I wondered what my first day would entail. I had practiced three different introductions. My daughter had told me to just be myself.

Here I was again! In Brooklyn! But this time it was different. I no longer took the subway, now I sat in my own seat on the Long Island Railroad. I had a suit on, not a jeans and t-shirt with thoughts of survival racing through my head. I still wasn't sure how I would introduce myself. I didn't even know who I was. The last time I took the train to Brooklyn I was homeless. And since moving to Queens, I never returned. The memories were too vivid. Now here I was, once again. This time it was different. This time I wasn't homeless. I had a home. I had a choice to drive my car to Brooklyn. I didn't *have to* take the train. Yes, this time *was* different indeed.

The train pulled off and I held my head down to avoid looking into the eyes of anyone. I wanted to be alone. Maybe I should have driven to Brooklyn. But I had heard how terrible parking was and wanted to avoid the hustle and bustle of downtown Brooklyn, New York. So many emotions raced through my body as I sat alone on the train. Would I be able to handle it – walking on Fulton Street once again? Would my emotions take over and break me down or would I be strong enough?
Years ago, I didn't even know I was being strong. I just knew I was surviving. Years ago, I didn't even know I was a number in the American system's statistics. I just knew life had happened and I just happened to get caught in the mix. But I have to admit I was strong then, and I will be strong now. I had to. I had no other choice.

Since coming to America I must have had over forty jobs . . . okay, a little exaggeration here, but many, many jobs, too many to count; none substantive except when I worked for the government, the bank, and a few hospitals. Now I was a professor, an assistant professor. Professor Richardson! I was not yet Dr. Richardson. Had not yet completed my doctorate in health administration. I was Prof. Richardson. Wow, had a nice ring to it. I had practiced my speech of how I would introduce myself to the students on the first day. The thought of it still had me puzzled. How did I get from being homeless to becoming a professor? How did I emerge from homelessness? How did I overcome the stigma of teenage pregnancy? How did I rid myself from the title, illegal alien? And how did I survive society's statistic of being raped, more so, raped only to find out I was pregnant? How did I find myself here? In this place, on the train, heading to Brooklyn to teach with the title professor? Looking back now it was a long journey indeed. But somewhere deep inside I knew if I told myself I could, I would. And I had to, so I did.

The train pulled into the station very slowly. My thoughts must have preoccupied my mind because I had not realized just how quickly the train had arrived at our destination, Atlantic Avenue. Everyone seemed anxious to exit the train. Everyone but me. I searched for my bag, picked up the copies of handouts I prepared the night before and made my way to the streets that awaited me. They welcomed me with open arms. The cool wind of October graced my face. And as if to say, *Welcome Home*, the wind caressed my hair, first gently, then seductively, and like a man in passion, became

aggressively impatient as each breath played with each strand of my hair.
Once outside the subway I had to take a bus to the college. I rejoiced within to know that the buses ran frequently. I had *just* missed a bus, but a couple of blocks away I saw another bus slowly making its way to Flatbush and Atlantic. Even the little engine that could went faster.

The ride was unusually quiet. That could be due to the fact it was 11 0'clock and students were already in class. Whatever the reason I was happy for the peaceful ride. It was soon my stop to exit the bus. I had forgotten to ring the bell alerting the driver I needed to get off. Thankfully a woman in the back was also exiting. The passengers' stares followed me as I made my way to the door to exit the bus. Once off the bus, I walked slowly, rehearsing my introduction.

A lot had changed. Macy's department store was at the location where A&S once was. That's where I had met Anita, the cashier at A&S from Panama. Anita had helped me when I needed assistance the most. I often wondered where she was, a stranger, who but for a quick moment served a purpose in my life. I searched for Wilfred's Academy, the beauty school, but that too no longer occupied the space where once it provided a learning environment for prospective beauticians. Now another building provided space for other businesses. That's when I realized the location of the college was at the exact same address I had my hair done by students as that was the only way I could afford a perm. The college where I would impart knowledge once occupied the business that permed my hair for several dollars which was all I could afford. Here I was, in Brooklyn, same location just twenty eight years later. I wasn't homeless. And though I was on a mission, this time, it was a different kind of a mission.

I entered the building and made my way to the second floor. The woman at the desk seemed so familiar. I knew her from somewhere. I made my way over to her desk and whispered, "Hi, good afternoon. My name is Karlene Richardson. I am the new prof . . . prof . . . professor." Yes, this would take some getting used to. I couldn't even say it right. "Hi, I'm Ms. Christopher, your desk is over there," she pointed to the far corner behind the water cooler.
"Thank you, do I know you from somewhere?" I knew I did, but just couldn't remember where I had seen her face before.
"No," she had an accent.
Jamaican, I bet she is Jamaican. I bet she lived somewhere close to me. I had to ask.
"Are you Jamaican?"
She smiled then answered, "No. I am from Trinidad. Not Jamaican."
"Okay, I'm sorry," I said apologizing.
"No need to apologize, and welcome."
"Thank you Ms. Christopher."

Above my desk was a name plate made of paper. It read: Prof. Richardson. I was still in awe. But I was thankful. I knew this had to be God!

I placed the handouts I made to distribute to my students on the desk and sat in the cheaply made seat. My mind slowly drifted again, and I just could not believe it . . . here I was in Brooklyn again . . .

But Who Was I Anyway?

Life had never been easy for me and therefore I had transformed into many different roles over the years since I left Jamaica. I even became a hustler just trying to pay my tuition and my rent. I worked in a Bank, I worked in retail; I worked at a temp agency for many, many years. Sometimes I worked in my own name, or other times I worked using fictitious names – whatever it took to put a roof over my daughter's head and food on the table. The only role I refused to play was a prostitute. I never could fathom that role! But I had even thought of pole dancing. But I never had the guts to do that either. It remained just a thought. Well the truth was I did try. But the man who owned the bar had said, "What are you doing here? You don't belong here . . . go find an education." I had shared the story with my Aunt Martha and we had laughed together. We shared many moments and that was one of them . . . me, a pole dancer. The thought was provoking enough for me to call the number in the ad I saw in the paper. Unfortunately the man refused to hire me and pointed me to education instead. And to think, I was really, really disappointed.

For years I struggled financially. For years I had no support. For many years I yearned to earn enough to provide for my children the way a mother ought to provide for her kids. I had tried to find someone who would love me and my daughter and whom we could love in return. For many, many, many years I had fantasized of being with a good man. For years that fantasy never came true.

It is a fact that we all yearn to be loved at one point or another. But sometimes the choices we make haunts us for life. Some are lucky enough to have chosen one partner who remained in their lives forever. Others like me, seems to try till we get it right.
I haven't been with many men still on my one hand counting, but yet one too many. I could blame my mother for not being there for me. But the real blame if I never found love would be me. Had I love myself enough? Had I approve of me instead of waiting on a man to give me the stamp of his approval. Had I lifted myself up sooner from the 'You'll never make it', or 'I'll live to see you in a shelter', or even the 'I wish I had aborted you', maybe just maybe I would have achieved more in life, earlier.

I knew I had not achieved anything but the realization came while watching the 'Oprah Winfrey' show titled *Millions by Millennium*. The show made me realize that I really had not achieved much of anything. Then I was thirty years old and had not accomplished much of anything. I did not have a home of my own, no proper luggage set, and no degree. Because according to the show, a woman is a woman when she has a house, a good set of luggage, and other items that showed her worth. Not sure if I agreed on all that, but I was sure brought to the realization that I had nothing. Nothing. I had a wonderful daughter. I had a job but not a career, and still did not know exactly what I wanted to do in life just yet.

I knew I had a purpose but exactly what it was only God knew. I knew among the many things I desired in life was love. I had read so many books that taught me how to love myself. How to invest in the self where loving self was concerned; How to make self first priority; I actually read a book that literally taught me that hugging self in the morning, staring self in the mirror, then telling self, *I love you self*, fulfilled an emptiness that dwelled within the soul. And that unless you fully relieved yourself of that emptiness, [and you could only do so by finding the reason for the emptiness], then you could never be fully satisfied as a person.

The book stated that no one in this world would ever be adequate enough to satisfy the craving of love desired. That no relationship you encountered would be sufficient, and that eventually you 'settled' for whomever and sometimes 'whatever'.

After reading 'THAT BOOK', I scrupulously searched my soul and my life completely. It seemed to me then, that I had been empty for thirty years. It seemed to me that I had 'settled' for whomever, and may I add whatever for a long, long time. But the truth was I had craved love for an extensive amount of time. I never did find it though.

I was married but that marriage was not built on or filled with love. At least not on my part. They were filled with 'for the children's sake'. Filled with 'for my pride's sake'. I stayed in the relationship mostly because of pride. Because I could not see me without the 'Mrs.' beside my name. I could not identify me without him. I could not bear to answer the *why's* and hear the *I'm sorry's*. I could not stand to even imagine having a failed marriage, because that meant *I* failed. At least that's what I thought. I stayed because people around me *expected* me to stay or because others looked on in silence hoping for us to not be together, and I wanted to prove them wrong. Furthermore, I couldn't fathom the thought of raising my children alone. Of dismantling the 'perfect family' image. The 'perfect couple' image. I stayed in the relationship because of my selfish pride. Of the emptiness I carried around for years without identifying it. Of the emptiness that caused me to overlook many of my fears of not knowing that *I* could make me happy. I could love me and not be thought conceited. I stayed because I could not and did not want to be alone again. I did not want to walk the streets of Brooklyn and not mean something to someone. I honestly stayed because I did not know the love I searched for could only come from within.

In the fifth year of my marriage to Doug I gave my life to the Lord. It was then that I found inner peace and ***true genuine love.*** An everlasting love. A kind of love that you know you have regardless of your faults, shape or weight. I found a friend that was a friend before I even knew how to be a friend to him. But the truth was, I still had a different kind of craving on the inside to be loved. My emptiness still lingered after the dogs stopped barking and the street lights came on. I could write that I was satisfied with the love I received from God. And I was because I found a new joy. But at nights when all lights went off, and my prayer reached 'AMEN', I craved a different kind of love.
You may not know the kind of love that I'm talking about because you're happily married. But I'm talking to all the sistas' and brothers' out there, regardless of your skin color that can relate.

I've *so* longed for that kind of love that illuminates a smile transversely on your face while going home, on the train or in your car, because you know it's love and you've finally found it. The kind of love that causes you to eat all kinds of junk yet, not feeling guilty about adding on a pound or two. The kind of love that when you look at yourself in the mirror, naked I might add, you know you look good, despite the hills and valleys uniquely created from fats and cellulites. I craved the kind of love that needed no reminder that it was Valentine's Day, Christmas Day or Birthday. 'Cause everyday was Valentine's, Christmas, and my Birthday.

I craved unconditional love. A love that you know you can return your all into it and know it's worth putting your all into. That *genuine* kind of love.

I soon wondered if my desire was a fantasy, and whether that kind of love existed at all. But I eventually learned the hard way that, that love existed. BUT it only exists after you've learned to love yourself and learned to prioritize YOUR needs selflessly. It only exists after learning that no one can do for you what only you can do for yourself. And that is to make *you* the most important factor in your life.

Through my experiences I learned that a marriage is not the road map to success or to finding love. You have to find love and have a road map leading to your success for yourself. The mistake I made? Thinking that a marriage will solve my dilemma - loneliness, emptiness, financial woes, and a desire for love. The only thing it brought? A companion to *share* my loneliness, emptiness, financial woes, and one also seeking for love.

I didn't find true happiness until I found myself. I didn't find love until I found the reason why I existed. I didn't fill the emptiness within until I fell in love with myself for the first time.

Those Were The Days of My Life . . .

I remembered the days laying on my sofa reminiscing about my past and about my marriage and realized that finding the Lord **was** the best thing that ever happened to me. Now with the strength of God, I was able to face the truth about my marriage. Although I still felt the same pain I felt years before, I had the strength to conquer my fears, and a rock to run to. Now joy was just a prayer away and peace only a song away.

My marriage was not regretful at first. Despite the reasons why I married Doug, it was a cradle to me after my relationship with my mother deteriorated. Then, Doug was the best thing that had happened to me since I left Jamaica. He worked and I stayed home. It is amazing how we cherish someone in the start of a relationship but hate the same person when things get disagreeable.

We all have motives for entering relationships and marriages. Yes we do! For some it's love, money, the fantasy of getting married - the white dress, the rock on the hand, the expressions of the well-wishers and the haters as we say 'I do' – the truth is, we all have motives. For me, well, it was definitely not for love. It couldn't have been. Thinking back now it was for everything else but love. If you ask me now why I married Doug I still haven't found the reason. I didn't even know what 'marriage' entailed. I didn't even know the terminologies of marriage - Truth, For Better, For Worst, Self, Individuality, etc.

Terminologies shouldn't change when marriage is entered into, they should be enhanced, not terminated. With Doug though, I didn't even know what the word marriage meant. But it served its purpose. I needed somewhere to stay after I got kicked out of my mother's house and was homeless for almost a year. I couldn't 'survive' anymore. I was tired and weak and worn. I had a baby to care for and was homeless and I was only eighteen years old. So when Doug came and 'rescued me', I was glad. At least I would have a place to call home, even if I was unhappy. I had a home. My daughter had a home. WE had a roof over our heads. And for whatever purpose it served, the purpose was well served because my daughter and I finally found comfort and a place of rest.

It took me a long time to appreciate Doug and the things he did for us despite the fact that he . . .

Love Me Tender

I have known you for so long
Yet I love you not.
Never spent the time to embrace the real you
Always searching, looking
Trying to find someone else.
Never satisfied.
But today here you are
Looking me dead in the eyes
A reflection of a never-loved child.
And all but suddenly
I love you.
All so quickly
I do know you.
So spontaneously
I recognize.
And finally
I am satisfied -
With who I am.
God's child.

CHAPTER 1

HOW IT STARTED ...

Since migrating from Jamaica to America, life was just not the same. Reality had sunk in that it would never be the same again. I was given to my grandfather and his wife when I was only eight months old. My older sister, Ilza, came to live with us shortly after, maybe six months later. Ilza and I grew up in a small section of Franklyn Town, in the city of Kingston, Jamaica. We lived on Lincoln Terrace, a quiet, dead-end street. My sister and I were pampered.

> The day to make my trip to the embassy finally arrived. I woke up early enough to take a long shower before beginning my journey. The water was freezing. I inhaled deeply and ran beneath its coldness against my skin, letting out a silent shriek.

My mother had six children, including me and my sister. She kept custody of her other four children whom she had for another man that she lived with. I never understood why Ilza and I weren't allowed to live with our mother but her other children did. It bothered me more than it did Ilza. Sometimes we sat on our veranda and fantasized what it would be like to have a mother instead of having our step grandmother, Sistermay. We loved Sistermay. She was an angel on earth. She cooked, cleaned, and cared for us as she would her own children. But we often wondered just what it would be like having a mother to care for us.

Sistermay never had any children of her own so we became her children. Even though she did so much for us we were always embarrassed to introduce her to our friends. Our friends' mothers were young with toned bodies. Sistermay was not. She was obese and in her fifties. Ilza and I wished for a mom whom we could be proud to introduce to our friends, but we never got our wish.

My mother migrated to the United States when I was twelve years old and Ilza was fourteen. Months after she left, I got baptized at the Pentecostal church I attended with our neighbors on Wildman Street. I learned about God, but I never took the time to know him personally, or to build a solid relationship with him. It was difficult living in a house where there were no Christian role models. But it was even more difficult with a sister who taunted and criticized the fact that I went to church. I eventually stopped going to church.

Our neighbors were The Carters, mother, father, four daughters and a son. We rarely saw the son, but the four daughters were Christians who took us to church. The eldest daughter, Dawn washed our hair and combed it. Dawn washed our hair totally different than Sistermay. Sistermay had us standing under the shower with the soap running down our faces. Ilza and I screamed whenever we had our hair washed. But when Dawn washed our hair, we were pampered. Dawn would lay us down on a make-shift bench in the back of their house. We lay on her lap with our faces to the ceiling. She would tilt our heads over the basin and tenderly massage the scalp. We often wondered why Sistermay did not wash our hair as Dawn did. We loved the four sisters. I wished to be one of the sisters in the family. They were always talking about heaven. I wanted to go to heaven so I decided to go to church with The Carters even when Ilza refused to go.

Attending church had taken my mind off the yearning I had deep within for a mother's love. After I stopped attending, the yearning returned. I wanted to see my mother. But I dare not ask Sistermay to take me to the embassy. She may have viewed me as ungrateful. And I loved Sistermay and would never want to hurt her. So I just did not ask her to take me to the Embassy. I made my own plans to go by myself.

As a child I was very advance academically for my age. I started high school at ten years old. So it was then not surprising to my grandmother that at thirteen years old I decided to go to the American Embassy for a Visa, by myself, without any parental support. Desperately, I asked Ilza to accompany me, but she refused. I was afraid to travel to the Embassy by myself. I had heard my grandmother talking to our neighbor who had recently received a Visa to travel to America. Our neighbor informed her that the lines of people waiting for Visas at the American Embassy were very long. For that reason, anyone wanting a Visa should arrive at the Embassy by 6 a.m. The streets were still dark at six o'clock. But, I was still determined to go despite knowing that at six o'clock, the cocks in the neighbor's backyard would just begin crowing, and there would be very few people on the streets. I was afraid of robbers and rapists. Ilza always said we lived in a bad community. However, the street we lived on was peaceful and quiet. It was not accessible to anyone unless you lived there or knew someone who did. It was a quiet and middle-class street in the ghetto.

The day to make my trip to the Embassy finally arrived. I woke up early enough to take a long shower before beginning my journey. The water was freezing. I inhaled deeply and ran beneath its coldness against my skin, letting out a silent shriek. My grandfather had left half an hour earlier for work. And so did my grandmother. We had a grocery store in an adjoining community, so she left early to open in time for those who came to buy bread, milk, sugar, and eggs to make breakfast for their children before sending them off to school. My grandfather had gotten promoted at his job and was expected at work earlier. He now wore a tie, shirt, and pants with dress shoes. He started out cleaning the pool for the resort where he worked. Seventeen years later, he was the assistant director.

My skin felt sore from the cold water I endured. I quickly got dressed. Ilza was still asleep when I went returned to our bedroom. I sat on the edge of my bed and lotioned my skin. I decided to use a little Vaseline, to keep my skin from looking dry.
"Ilza," I whispered. But she did not answer. "Ilza," I repeated.
"What?!" She replied angrily. She hated when I woke her up from her sleep but I didn't care. At least not this morning.
"I'm leaving now, are you coming?"
She eased her face off her pillow and turned her face towards me, "Going where?"
"To the Embassy, remember?" I asked, still hoping she

would change her mind.

"Misses gwaan and lef' me alone, I don't know if you t'ink dem wid give *you* a Visa. Yuhh mad?" ... Nuh baddy wid gi visa to nuh 13 year old >>> [Listen, go and leave me alone. Do you really think they are going to give you a Visa. Are you crazy? ... No one will give a visa to a 13 year old.]

I could tell she was very serious. I wanted to take my uniform off and wiggle my way beside her on her bed beneath the warm sheets. But I resisted and instead decided to go alone.

As I walked away, I held my head down and thought that maybe Ilza did have a point. Why would they give a thirteen year old a visa without parental consent? I wanted to not go and jump in bed instead, but my pride would not allow me to deviate from my plans. I still intended to go.

"Okay, bye." Even though I said bye I wished for her to come. But she remained asleep and didn't say a word. She must have known that I still stood beside her bed.

"Mmm," she barely responded.

As I made my way to the bus stop the fear I felt intensified. I decided to wear my high school uniform to show the workers at the Embassy that I was a student. I had a letter that I had written myself as though my uncle's wife had written it. I had placed it in the envelope from a letter she had written to my grandmother. I was not sure what made me more anxious, the fear of traveling alone in the darkness of the morning, or the lie I was about to tell the person at the window at the Embassy.

I decided to take the van instead of the bus. I would get there much quicker. As I waited on the dark and lonely street, the van seemed to take forever to come. But when it came it was empty, and only because it was six o'clock in the morning. The vans are usually crowded that the conductor of the van usually hangs half way out the door. I made my way in and tried to conceal my fear. The morning air was crisp. The few passengers remained silent. The drive seemed longer than it really was. Then finally it was my turn to get off. As I made my way to the Embassy I wondered what it would be like to really get a visa and to really live with my mother. I had not told anyone, but that was the real reason I wanted a visa. I wanted to be with my mom. I loved Sistermay and my granddaddy, but I wanted my mother.

The lines at the Embassy were not as long as our neighbor had said. But soon after I arrived, more people came in droves. We were given papers to fill out while we waited. We watched a documentary of something. I wasn't interested so I didn't watch. All I could think of was Ilza and my mother. Why hadn't Ilza come? Didn't she want to be with our mother as well? She always said she wished our mother loved us enough to want to be with us. And now we had a chance and she refused. But I decided to go anyway.

I daydreamed the entire time I waited. I daydreamed about America. I daydreamed of the nice things I would buy for Ilza. I daydreamed of the wonderful time I would spend with my mom, finally.

Soon it was my turn to see an Immigration Officer. The lady at 'Window 3' beckoned me towards her.
"Hello," she had a wide grin and the lipstick she had on decorated her teeth.

"Hi," my voice cracked from anxiety.
"How may I help you? Your passport please."
I handed her my passport before telling her I wanted to visit my aunt. I knew better than to say mother.
"Where are your mom and dad?" Her voice was mellow and her accent different from ours.
"At work," I lied.
"And you want to go to the U.S. right? You just want to see what it's like? Aren't you in school? Will you be out then?"
She asked so many questions. I was glad Ilza wasn't here because she surely would tell her she asked too many questions. Ilza wasn't afraid to tell anybody anything. She spoke her mind. Sometimes too much.
"Yes I would like to go and see what it's like."
"Okay then, come and pick up your passport after three o'clock this evening. And enjoy your stay in America. I hope you will get to see the snow while you're there. It's beautiful."
"Thank you Ma'am."
"You're welcome. Enjoy okay."
I couldn't believe she gave me a visa. Everyone on the line behind me looked in disbelief. I was ecstatic. I felt as though I wanted to run home. I couldn't wait to reach home to tell Ilza the good news.
Then I suddenly remembered I would be leaving Ilza behind. She would not be able to come unless she tried to get a visa too.
I hopped on the first van even though it was packed and seemed illegal to fit even one more passenger. Anxiety almost killed me. The ride home took forever - or so it seemed. Finally I was walking towards my house. My feet could not carry me quickly enough. I quickly opened the gate and banged on the grilled gate that

secured our house.

"What?!" Ilza shouted as she came to open the lock on the gate.

"I got it!" Handing her the paper the lady gave me to claim my passport in the evening.

"Yeah right," she took the paper and observed it.

I could tell she felt like fainting because her face looked flushed.

"Yuhh lucky," >>> [Good for you] was all she could say before sitting and just staring at me before she continued, "so when yuhh will leave?" >>> [So when are you leaving?]

"A don't know yet. A didn't even tell Sistermay and Daddy yet."

We never said granddaddy, we always called him 'Daddy'.

Minutes later I called the grocery store and told Sistermay. Then I called Daddy and told him. They were both happy. But they couldn't understand how I managed to get a visa at thirteen without any parents being present. But I did. Daddy said I was always special. I started high school at ten years old. I went to first, second, and third grade. Then when I returned to school the following September they promoted me to the fifth grade instead of the fourth grade. When I returned to school after Christmas break instead of returning to the fifth grade, I was placed in the sixth grade. I took the promotion test, Common Entrance, and passed. I was only ten years old. And now at thirteen years old, I had somehow managed to convince the Immigration Officer to grant me a visa. So daddy said he knew I was always 'special'.

Ilza and I watched the clock until it was time for me to return to the Embassy to pick up my passport with the visa. Ilza followed me back to the Embassy to get my passport. On our way back from the Embassy she decided that in the morning she too would go to the Embassy. I was excited. Maybe now we would both go to see our mother and then we would live happily with her.

That night when Daddy and Sistermay came home, we all celebrated. We called my mother to tell her the good news. I was shocked by my mother's response. She sounded disappointed instead of being happy. But I was too excited for it to matter then. They both decided on the date that I should leave and made arrangements to buy the ticket and clothes for me to wear.

The next day I followed Ilza to get her visa. But she was denied. The man at the window said Ilza needed her mother or father to accompany her. She almost asked the Immigration Officer why then was her sister granted a visa at thirteen years old and she was denied a visa at fifteen years old? Ilza was two years older than me. I was glad she hadn't asked the Immigration Officer the question to clarify why she wasn't granted a visa, because they may have revoked mine.

CHAPTER 2

JOURNEY TO MY DESTINY...

The days came quickly for me to leave. As I packed my clothes in the suitcase that I borrowed from my grandmother, I knew I would miss Ilza terribly. I still could not believe the day for my departure was finally here. Ilza and I had spoken about me leaving almost every day. Now it was finally here. Each time we spoke about my upcoming trip I tried hard not to cry as we spoke. And each time I tried, a huge gulp formed in my throat.

> Sistermay was the first to hug me. She was also the first to start crying. Then I hugged Ilza and we both started crying. Ilza held onto me and wouldn't let me go. I did not want to let her go either. But I had to go. We both bawled and hugged each other for several minutes.

Ilza and I had written a long list of the things she wanted me to buy in America. She joked throughout the entire journey to the airport. That was her way of not thinking about me leaving. I remained silent, laughing at all her jokes, even the ones that weren't funny. Looking at her I wondered if I would ever see her again. Because deep within I knew I wouldn't return to Jamaica. I wanted to live with my mother. I would miss Ilza, but I so needed my mother's love.

Ilza was all I had and I was all she ever had. But here we were ready to say goodbye not knowing if we would ever see each other again. We were always close as sisters, but we were even closer as friends. I was

anxious and fearful at the same time. Walking slowly, I picked up my suitcase and placed it on the scale at the Air Jamaica ticket counter. The woman stood about five feet two inches tall barely seeing above the counter. She took my ticket and checked to make sure I was who I said I was.
"Is this all?" She asked referring to the piece of luggage.
"Yes Ma'am."
"Did you pack your luggage yourself?"
"Yes Ma'am."
"Did anyone give you anything to carry in your luggage?"
"No." I thought her questions ridiculous. Why would I take anything from anyone to carry on the plane?
"Okay. Your gate is 17 and it leaves in forty-five minutes. Be on time."
I returned to Ilza and Sistermay who stood across from the counter talking. This was it. I had to go. This was as far as Ilza and Sistermay were permitted to follow me. This is where I would have to say goodbye. Sistermay was the first to hug me. She was also the first to start crying. Then I hugged Ilza and we both started crying. Ilza held onto me and wouldn't let me go. I did not want to let her go either. But I had to go. We both bawled and hugged each other. Then I wondered why I had even bothered to go to the Embassy. I had a good family. So why was I leaving them to go to the unknown?
I loved my sister and I knew she loved me. We were all we ever had.

Our father had left Jamaica when Ilza was only two years old and I was only several months old. He lived in America since then. He took very good care of us. I never knew what career he had, but he took very good care of us. When I had passed the Common Entrance test, my father had sent a suitcase filled with clothes, shoes, and jewelry as a congratulatory gift for me. He frequently sent money to Sistermay to care for us. We spoke to him sometimes on the phone. I can't remember ever hearing my biological father tell me that he loved me. But I knew he did because of the way he took care of us. I never heard those words from anyone other than my granddaddy. I heard it every night before I fell asleep. No matter how late my granddaddy came home from work he came in my bedroom to say "Mitchy, I love you and good night." To my family, I was Michelle. To my classmates, I was Karlene. But to my daddy, I was Mitchy.

Two years before I got my visa, Ilza and I got news that our father died. He was shot once in the head at the intersection of Nostrand and Flatbush Avenues. It was only then that we knew our father's career. Our father was a member of a Jamaican posse, The Untouchables, a gang from the 1970's. So were several of my uncles and cousins along with their friends. We finally found out many things about our father. He sold drugs and lots of it. It all made sense. That's how he was able to afford the luxury he provided for us. When other children took five dollars or less to school for lunch, Ilza and I took twenty dollars. Not only were we cared for. We were spoiled.

I knew I had to go to Gate 17, but with Ilza still crying, how could I? And so was Sistermay. I was too embarrassed to cry. Daddy chose not to come to the airport to say bye. He had hugged me before he left for work in the morning and begged me to take care of myself. I knew if he had come he would have cried although we have never seen daddy cried before. I eventually broke free from Ilza's arms. I somehow managed to say goodbye and walked away, not looking back. I could still hear Ilza's cry. I also heard Sistermay telling her to stop crying now because I would be back in a month. But deep within I knew I would not return. I entered through the metal detectors and scanned my bag. The custom officers gave me permission to proceed to the waiting area. I soon disappeared from view behind a wall that separated me from Ilza, Sistermay, Daddy, and my home of love and comfort.

Minutes after I arrived at the waiting area, it was time for me to board the plane. Once again my ticket was checked and I was allowed to board the plane. As I walked briskly towards the big Air Jamaica plane I looked up and saw my grandmother and my sister both waving goodbye from behind the gated balcony atop the airport. My eyes were quickly swollen with tears and the huge bulge returned in my throat as I tried hard to swallow. I tried as hard as I could to fight back the tears, but they flowed like the river over troubled water. I was embarrassed for anyone to see my tears but I could no longer control the flow. I had held them back as I said goodbye to Ilza. But now, I couldn't hold them back any more.
As I settled in my seat and buckled my seat belt, my eyes wandered around the huge bus-like transportation. I could not see what all the excitement was about an airplane and everyone wanting to travel on one. The airplane was nothing but a big bus with wings. Maybe all the excitement came from leaving a small island and

wandering off to an unknown place.
As it began down the runway, I allowed the tears to finally flow as I looked through the window. I tried to see if I could identify Ilza from amongst the many people standing on the balcony, but she was too far away.
Would I ever see Ilza again? Had I made the right decision? Maybe I should have never gone without her to the Embassy. But I knew it was too late now. The tears flowed heavier and the bulge in my throat grew bigger, which made it difficult and painful to swallow. I knew I would miss her very much. I knew she would miss me too. She had cried so much as she said goodbye. I knew my sister loved me, but I had not known just how much. Why hadn't she come with me to the Embassy? Why did I go without her? Staring into the emptiness of the sky beyond the wings of the plane, I searched the clouds in amazement, trying desperately to hide my face from anyone seeing my tears.

I slept through most of the journey. The flight attendant woke me up for dinner. The food tasted wonderful and the drink, whatever it was, was very good. I wanted to ask for more, but I was too shy. I must have fallen asleep again, because I was awakened by the sounds of clapping hands. Looking through the window, I saw we had landed. Everyone clapped. The lady beside me thanked God for a safe landing. I guess that justified the clapping. We sat for what seemed like forever before we were allowed to exit the plane.
I followed the crowd to an open area where our luggage was. As I fumbled through the luggage to reach my suitcase I stumbled over a huge case of rum. My suitcase was not heavy. I had not packed too many

things, because I was coming to 'glory land'. Or so I thought. I anxiously waited for my turn to approach the man at the desk. Then it was my turn. The man behind the desk was Caucasian. I had never before been so close to a white man before. The only other time was at the Embassy, but the Caucasian woman stood behind the glass window. Now here I was so close. His skin looked pale in some areas and deep red in other areas on his face. His accent was deep. His eyes were blue, almost like the sky beneath the wings of the plane.
He asked for my passport and asked how long I would stay. I told him about a month. He stamped the page in my passport and wished me a good experience. Never before had I seen so many white people.

As I struggled towards the door leading to the exit, I hoped that I would somehow recognize my uncle, my mother's brother. He had left Jamaica when I was only three months old. But we received many pictures from him. He never returned to visit, he only sent money and called at least once per week. He too was a part of the Untouchables.
As soon as the electronic door opened, I saw his face amidst the crowd.
"Wha'pen?">>>(What happen?) he asked, and then continued before waiting to get an answer. "Was the flight long?" This time he paused and looked at me waiting for an answer, as he took my suitcase.
"No," I answered shyly looking at the floor to avoid his eyes. I couldn't believe I was in the presence of Michael. He was our family's idol. He had a lot of money just like my father did. I could not believe I was actually here with Uncle Michael.
He led me to his car, which was parked outside the exit

of the airport terminal. He assisted me with my suitcase and helped me in his car. We didn't have a car in Jamaica. I had been in a car before but only cabs. This was the first time actually driving in a 'regular' car. The ride to my mother's house seemed long. America seemed big, extremely big. There were so many cars, and the streets were so wide and so long. It seemed like the streets never ended. And the noise from the horns were deafening. This was New York. Yes, this was the big apple that everyone craved for, and I was finally here for my slice so I could share it equally with my sister, Ilza. At the thought of her my eyes welled up with tears again and the bulge began to reappear. My uncle did not talk throughout the entire ride. The silence killed me. Eventually I did not know where to put my hands or where to allow my eyes to stare. I knew I had to break it, or I would keep thinking about Ilza and the tears would definitely flow, embarrassing me.

"How is Janet?" Janet was his daughter who came to visit us sometimes in Jamaica.

"She's okay, she's in school," he answered, not taking his eyes off the road.

He resembled my grandfather so much. He was his first son. And when he spoke, he sounded just like him too. Janet had come almost every Summer to visit us in Jamaica. Whenever she came, everyone idolized her. After all, she was a 'foreigner'. I couldn't wait to see her. The car pulled up slowly to the curb of a street in Brooklyn.

"Si yuhh madda dere," >>> [There's your mother] Uncle Michael said pointing to a window on the apartment building. Her face was pressed against the window of an apartment on the first floor. As I stepped out the car, a frigid air brushed my face. It was freezing cold, to me that was. Apparently it was not too cold for my uncle because he only had on a light jacket and a baseball cap. It was the twenty-eighth day in April, but I was extremely cold.

After he took me in he stayed for about half of an hour to get his share of Jamaican products that Sistermay had sent. She had sent fried fish, bammy, thyme, and a few mangoes. She had hid them very well. Fortunately, the custom officer had not checked my luggage. My uncle said if they had checked the luggage they would have confiscated the mangoes and thyme.

Where am I going?

Where am I going?
What is my goal?
To which tribe do I belong?
Am I forsaking the land that birth me?
Am I forsaking my tribe?
'Tis a journey that holds destiny
A journey to the heart of the old
To the place where wise men traveled
A place where experiences are told.
A journey where I heard the streets
are all lined with gold.
An old wife's fable?
Could be.
Yet I journey.
And so I journey.

CHAPTER 3

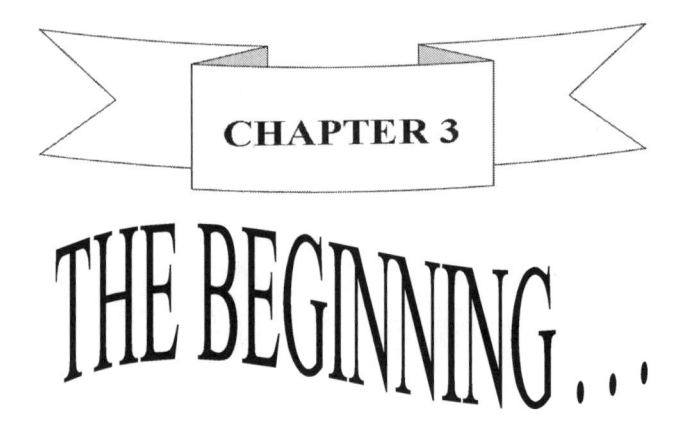

THE BEGINNING...

My mother's apartment was small. It had one bedroom, a bathroom, and a shared space for the kitchen and living room. I learned quickly that the living room was my bedroom. The pull-out sofa was my bed. In the mornings she expected me to fold up the bed so the living room would be kept proper. I was introduced formally to her husband, Mike. I had seen him before in Jamaica at a party that was kept at our house. He had stayed briefly. He was tall and handsome. He seemed mild mannered. I was also introduced to my little brother, Dave, who was six months old. Several months after my mother left Jamaica, her husband, who was her fiancé then, followed. Months later they got married. Uncle Michael had helped to pay for her wedding. Now here she was with a new family. I wondered how I would fit in this equation. Maybe this was the reason Ilza chose to stay. After Ilza and I were given to our grandparents my mother had started a new family. She had four children, two boys and two girls. Ilza always told me she loved them but never loved us. Eventually I saw the truth. After that relationship failed, she began dating Mike. Now here she was with yet another family. At first when she came to America, she sent shoes and clothes and barrels of food for us. The

> His weight was unbearable as he stripped himself of his clothes while laying on me to prevent me from moving about as I continued to do. Soon, he was naked also.
> I could feel his

majority of things went to my three brothers and sister. But soon after Mike came and she started her new family, things changed. We received less until eventually we seldom received anything at all.

My two youngest brothers were only six and eight years old when she left Jamaica. Eventually they stopped attending school. My grand aunt with whom they lived could no longer afford lunch for them.

After my uncle left, my mother and I got a chance to talk. I had never sat down to talk with my mother before. She was beautiful. She was a dark-skinned African queen. Her eyes were like pearl. Her lips held the words that I longed to hear. Her heart held the love that I longed to feel. Her arms bore the embrace that should have comforted me since birth. And I long to feel a mother's love. I wanted to hug her but something prevented me for I have never been held by this woman called mother. And I heard nothing she said because I was yearning and hurting for her love.
"Did you hear me?"
"Ah, no."
"I said, I have a friend who has a husband who works at Burger King in Manhattan. He said to bring you on Wednesday to fill out an application. Maybe you can work."
"Okay."
I was amazed. I had just gotten off the plane and here she was telling me I had to start working. I was only thirteen. But she said her friend's husband would fix it so I would have a social security number and be the right age to work. So many thoughts scattered throughout my mind. How would I get to work. But my question was

quickly answered as though she read my mind. She would show me the way the first day but then I was on my own.
My little brother finally awoke. He was gorgeous. I held him against my chest. He felt warm. I had never held a baby before so I was a little timid to do so.
That night I was allowed to call Jamaica and spoke with Ilza and Sistermay. Daddy was not home as usual. He was still at work. I really missed Ilza. My hurt ached as I said goodbye.

I couldn't believe my mother had made sure to find a job for me before I arrived in New York. My mother did take me to Burger King and I was hired. She accompanied me the first two days to the job. After that I was on my own. So three days after I arrived, I started working in Burger King as a cashier. Her friend's husband was the general manager. He hired me part time, even though I didn't have a green card. I worked from six o'clock in the morning to two o'clock in the evening. Sometimes I worked later. She told me I needed a job to buy whatever I needed. She also told me it would be nice if I could help to take care of my sisters. And of course there was nothing better than being 'nice'. I wanted to be loved so I would have done anything to be considered 'nice' to gain my mother's love.
But it seemed the more I tried the more she remained a stranger.
 Since I had come to live with her in New York, the only things she ever bought me was a sweater and a pair of jeans. Nothing more. The day after I arrived she took me downtown Brooklyn and I bought a sneakers, night

gown, jeans, and t-shirt with the fifty dollars I traveled with.

With the little money I worked at Burger King, I bought my sisters clothes and shoes.

Each morning, I took the train from Prospect Park at 5:00 am and got off at Fulton Street in Manhattan at 5:50 am. I then walked two blocks to the restaurant. Every morning, by myself, I walked alone on the streets of Brooklyn to the train station. The streets were lonely, but I knew I had to do it. My mother had made it clear that I had two choices - work or school. But judging by the way she had made it clear that she needed help with my sisters – she wanted me to work.

I would have done anything to please her to gain her love, but not even that was sufficient to gain her love.

I enjoyed working at Burger King more than I thought I would. Jeanette, my coworker, and I became close friends. When we were not at work we spoke frequently on the phone. Sometimes we hung out at South Street Seaport in Manhattan. Other times we just sat behind the restaurant and talked about boys, life, and the way my mother treated me. She always had a cigarette in her mouth when she was not working. And when she was not smoking she had a foil paper with white stuff sniffing through her nose. I never knew what it was until I asked. She said it was 'coke' that she bought for $25.00. I had never heard of 'coke' before. In Jamaica, I knew they had 'weed', but I had never heard of 'coke'. My aunt, Martha, had given me a puff of her 'weed' or 'spliff' she had called it when I was twelve. But since then I never tried it again. And like our president, I never inhaled. Really, I didn't. I didn't know how to. Jeanette had offered me cigarettes before, and I had tried it once. I hated it. It left a nasty taste in my mouth.

Then she offered me the white stuff in the foil paper, but I refused. I couldn't fathom pulling something through my nostrils. I often wondered if it was possible that you could actually drown from putting things up in your nose. I must admit I was naive. But that's how I grew up, sheltered by my grandparents. Well, until I came to live with my mother.

I was always in the house, except for the times I went to work, because I had no friends. Whenever I wasn't working, I baby sat Dave. My mother told me that I had to help out and that meant babysitting whenever she had to go out. She taught me to cook. I had to cook whenever she was not home. I had to make sure her husband had food to eat whenever he came home. Soon after emigrating from Jamaica to America it became obvious that my mother had only wanted me here with her to baby-sit Dave. I missed Ilza but the truth was I *did* not want to go back home either. I preferred living in America.
I still yearned for a mother's love. I came to America to find it, and I would not leave without it.

My mother constantly complained that I was always in the house, and introduced me to one of her friend's daughter, Dawn. Or she would allow me to go to the night club two blocks away with my paternal aunt. Or to sit outside with one of our neighbors daughter. Or sometimes she allowed me to go on trips with my aunt. Anything to get me out of the house.
Her friend's daughter, Dawn and I mostly spoke on the telephone. I preferred to stay in the house. My grandfather never allowed us to go out, so that is all I was used to doing - staying in the house. But my mother

thought differently. Maybe she wanted to be in the house with her new 'family', and I was an hindrance. So to get rid of me, she was glad whenever Dawn asked if I was allowed outside. The answer was always yes. But Dawn only came by whenever she wanted me to accompany her to visit her male friends. Dawn was two years older than I was.

On one of our visits to her male friends, she introduced me to a boy, Paul. We had gone to visit her friend Christopher, on Lincoln Place in Brooklyn, and that's where I met Paul. He was sitting on the last step of the stairs amidst four other males. I later learned they were his nephews. He beckoned me to sit beside him, which I gladly did. I was very shy and did not care to walk all the way up the steps. So I was glad to sit anywhere, beside anyone. After an hour of talking about nothing we exchanged numbers. I wasn't brave enough to say no. I did not have the guts to tell him 'Hell no.' So instead, I gave him my number. Anyway, my mother wouldn't care.

Paul was the first boy I had met since I lived in America. I was not interested in boys. His personality seemed much different than any other boy I had known. He was short, petite and light skinned. He was a total charmer. He was very bold and very mature in his conversations. He was four years older than I was.

Two days before his birthday, he came by Dawn's house while I was there visiting. He told Dawn he was having a 'get-together'. He invited us to his house for his 'get-together'. I was bit hesitant, but Dawn quickly convinced me to go. I informed my mother of the party. She agreed once I told her that Dawn would be there. I think she would have agreed regardless.

I had taken off the day from work. I got ready in my

white jeans, and a purple blouse, and went to meet Dawn. I had practiced all the dances, especially the whop, because I knew Dawn danced very well. I must have pressed the bell a million times before it was answered. Her mom answered the intercom and said she had left already. Disappointed, I returned home.
It must have been an half an hour after I returned home, before the phone rang. It was Paul. He sounded surprise to know I was still home. He questioned whether I had changed my mind. The music blasted in the background, which made it difficult for me to hear him clearly. Ignoring what he was saying, I interjected and asked if Dawn had already arrived. But the music drowned my question.
"Is Dawn there already?" I repeated.
"Not yet," he hesitated amidst his answer.
"Oh." I was disappointed to know Dawn had left without me. But I was even more disappointed to know she still had not arrived at Paul's house yet. I knew if I intended to enjoy the party, I had to reach early. My mother expected me back by 12:00 am.
"So are you coming?"
"Okay," I paused before asking him where he lived.
Even with the instructions he gave, I had no clue how to get to his house. He offered to pay a cab and gave me the directions to tell the driver.
Even as I waited for the cab I was still hesitant about leaving my house. I no longer felt like going after all Dawn had left without me. Eventually the cab came and reluctantly I began my journey to Paul's house to meet Dawn.
As the cab approached his house, I saw Paul standing patiently at the door. He approached the cab and paid the driver then escorted me into his house that was above

a grocery store.
"The music is loud," I complained.
"Oh that's not loud," he said smiling.
Entering the apartment I couldn't help noticed how nicely designed his apartment was. His apartment was dark with candles lit on top of the counter. It had a woman's touch. But I dare not ask. I wasn't interested anyway. I mean I did like him, but that's where it ended. As I went further into his apartment I was appalled. No one was there just me and Paul. There was no party. There was no Dawn. I felt like a fool. I couldn't believe I had been so stupid to believe there really was a party. He really played me. I wanted to go back home, but I was broke. I did not even have a quarter to make a phone call. Suddenly I remembered Dawn, had she known that there really wasn't a party? Was she in on this too?
"Can I leave?" I asked politely.
"Suh quick?" >>> [So quick?] he asked.
"Where's the party Paul?" I asked rolling my eyes at him in disgust. I really had started to like him. But after this stunt, I would never call him or Dawn. After this I would never accept any call from him either.
I decided to calm down. I didn't know if I could trust him. I suddenly felt scared. What had I gotten myself into? My heart raced against my chest. I wanted to leave.
"Paul I cannot stay, I have to leave," I tried to sound as brave as I could, faking it as I made my way to the door.
"Come on nuh man, why?" >>> [Come here, why?] he asked as he grabbed my arm in a friendly way.
"Please . . .I have to leave. I have to leave Paul," I started pleading.
But the look in his eyes told me he wanted me to stay. I

decided to not argue or beg. I would just play along. Maybe he would let me leave after he had his fair share of game.

I inhaled deeply then sat on his sofa. After lowering the music, he sat beside me.

I thought, 'good, maybe he just wanted to talk'. Then I would leave right after. Silently I prayed that God would see me through. I begged God to just let me leave safely and I promised never again to enter another man's house. I began feeling nauseous from anxiety. I still could not believe he had lied to me that he was having a birthday party. I still could not believe I had been so naïve.

"Want someting fi drink?" >>> [Would you like something to drink?]

I wanted to say no thank you, but I needed something to wet my dry throat, which had gotten dry from the anxiety attack I still experienced.

"Thank you," I managed to mutter as I tried to hide my fears.

As he walked towards the fridge, I observed him with disgust. I no longer liked him. In fact, I wished him dead.

"Yuhh okay now, si seh mi nah gu kill yuhh? Yuhh 'fraid ah man?" >>> [Are you okay now? Now you see that I'm not a killer? Are you afraid of men?], he interrogated as he handed me the drink.

Ignoring him and his questions I took a huge gulp. The drink was sweet, but within three minutes of listening to him telling me of his son in Jamaica, I had gulped every bit down.

His son was two years old. He had fallen madly in love with his son's mother despite the fact that her family resented him and thought him not good enough for her.

A year after he left Jamaica, she started dating someone else. He said she succumbed to her family's wishes. I had my own opinion. With a man like you, who wouldn't date someone else. He said he had taken good care of his son's mother. But that must not have been enough to keep her from being with another man. Not once did he mention her name. And I never asked. I wasn't interested. Amidst his sentences I began feeling dizzy. The entire room started to sway. He must have noticed, because he started coming closer. I had alcohol before but had never felt this way before. I was sure that's what he had given me. My head felt lighter. The room swayed more before my eyes. My thoughts went back to Dawn. I hated her now more than ever. How could she have set me up like this? She must have known he was not having a party, because they were her friends and furthermore she still was not here.

As he came closer he firmly placed his lips against mine securing my head against his with his hand to make sure I couldn't move. His lips felt warm against mine. I had never kissed anyone before. The thought of his saliva in my mouth made me furious. My mind said "Push him away," but my arms couldn't move. I wanted to run, but my feet were cemented into his floor. At least that's what it felt like. I managed to turn my head away, but my resistance was low because of the alcohol. I could feel his hand exploring my body, but was too weak to resist. I started to scream, but he placed one hand on my lips and kept telling me to stop acting like a child. I eventually succumbed to his wishes because my mind lost the will to fight.

I felt his hand pulling me off the sofa. I tried pulling away but his firm grip on my arms tugged me harder towards another room. My body swayed lifelessly at

each tug. Eventually he had gotten me to the place where he wanted. He lay me down on what appeared to be a bed. My body lay lifeless beneath his weight. His tongue explored my mouth and then my ears. His tongue wandered beneath my neck and made its way to my breast. I hit his head as hard as I could. Why was he doing this to me? Why was he exposing my body to his eyes? Wasn't this rape?
He started removing my clothes. Something from my clothes bruised my lips as it passed above my head. Intent on getting his way, he ignored my groan from the pain. Then with one hand he unhooked my bra and explored my womanliness. I felt ashamed and embarrassed. He was seeing me half naked. Then as if he read my mind, he pulled my underwear from my body. I fought as hard as I could but he insisted on getting his way. I was totally naked. I was naked in front of a man! Oh my God!
His weight was unbearable as he stripped himself of his clothes while laying on me to prevent me from moving about as I continued to do. Soon, he was naked also. I could feel his manhood against me. I hated him! I hated Dawn! I hated everything about America. I wanted to go home. My thoughts were suddenly interrupted by a fierce pain. My brain shattered. My heart beat escalated! Suddenly, I felt like I was about to be comatose. He suddenly stopped. My pain caused my groans to increase. I felt his hand caressing my head and him whispering he's sorry. But the pain was too intense for me to care about anything else. Then I knew nothing more.
I was startled in the morning to find myself naked beside a man I didn't know. I had never slept with a man before. My head felt groggy. Nothing made sense at

that moment. I could not focus long enough to think. I
drifted off to sleep again. Once again, I was awakened
by his hand across my chest. I glanced at the clock, it
said 10:00. I wasn't sure if it was p.m. or a.m. I prayed
that it was still night. But I was informed of the time
when he sat up and said, "Good Morning."
My mother would kill me.
"Hi," he whispered, as he rolled over. "Yuhh is a virgin.
Why yuhh neva tell me? Yuhh know how long mi a
wake yuhh up. Look here, mi sorry. Mi neva know.
Jesus Christ! A wey mi get mi self inna. How old yuhh
is?" >>> [You're a virgin?! Why didn't you tell me?
Do you know how long I've been trying to wake you up?
Listen, I'm very, very sorry. I didn't know. Oh my
God, what have I done? What have I gotten myself into.
By the way, how old are you anyway?]
I could tell he was genuinely sorry. But it was too late.
His apology didn't matter now. He took a gift from me
that I had wanted to give the man I decided to spend the
rest of my life with. I couldn't stop the tears from
flowing, they just came. I turned away feeling
embarrassed, as I used his comforter to cover my shame.
I was still in a daze. I still did not know just what had
happened. The last thing I remembered was drinking the
drink he gave me.
"Can I have a towel?" I said with the worst attitude ever.
My grandfather would kill me to know what I allowed to
happen to me. He never approved of us having 'friends'.
I never understood the reason. But from where I was,
somewhere in Brooklyn, I understood just perfectly.
I managed to wrap the towel around me without
exposing myself. As I sat up, my knees felt weak. I
desperately needed to empty my bladder. Squatting over
the toilet, I began to urinate, but I managed to stop the

flow after an excruciating pain raced through my reproductive organs. My body felt sore. I attempted to urinate again, but the pain got worse. Wetting a piece of tissue, I place it against my womanhood before attempting to urinate again, but that didn't help. The burning was too much to bear. I began to inhale and exhale deeply. Tiny trickles of urine flowed, though I tried to hold it back. I could no longer hold it back. Tightly I closed my eyes and urinated as fast as possible. The pain was excruciating. My heart was weak from the pain. My breathing increased, and so did the pain from the aftermath. I no longer cared whether sixty women sat on his toilet seat. I slowly lowered myself on the seat. I was shivering from the pain. Reaching slowly to get my underwear that had fell to my ankles, I was petrified to see blood on it.

I decided to take a shower maybe that would help the pain.

It was a task just getting in the tub. As I got in the bath, I glanced at myself in the mirror. I had a big red spot on my neck. 'That dog put it there,' I thought to myself. As the water ran over my body it soothed the outer part of my hurting soul. I deliberately avoided putting soap on my lower body fearing the pain that I would feel. Just then my mind wandered to what Paul had done to me throughout the night. I had wanted to save myself for someone who I would truly love. But now it was gone, forever. Tears ran down my face, though it became lost amidst the water that soothed me. I realized then that I was the tear amidst the water that flowed that suddenly became lost in this great big city.

In this big city who would notice me? Who cared enough anyway? I needed someone to talk to. But who could I tell? I had no friends.

I was startled by a loud bang that came from the other room. I quickly turned the water off and slowly got out of the tub. Slowly, I got dressed. Just as I was about to leave the bathroom, I heard voices. The voice sounded familiar. I recognized Dawn's voice. How could I face her? The nerve of her showing up now. I was convinced now more than ever that she knew there would be no party. I guess she was happy now that she must know Paul had his way with me. I wish them both hell in their lives.

"Is she here?" I could hear her asking Paul. I also heard her telling him my mother and stepfather had visited her house looking for me. I had told my mother that I would be going to a party with Dawn. Now it seemed as if I lied.

"She's here," he answered. Then he lowered his voice. I couldn't hear what he was saying. But from the look on her face after I opened the bathroom door making my way to his bedroom where I left my clothes, I could tell he had told her what had happened. I tried to act as though everything was okay. But it was not. I wanted to tell Dawn, but she was not a friend. I know I could not tell my mother, she would kill me. How could he have taken my gift of a lifetime in just one night?

By the time I returned to the living room Dawn had left. Paul was washing the glass I drank out of. I wondered how many girls he had done this to before. I grabbed my bag from the chair where I placed it the night before. He handed me a twenty dollar bill for the cab and told me it was on the way. I felt like a real whore. A real twenty-dollar-whore. I had wanted to throw it in his face, but I needed it to pay the cab and I had no idea where in Brooklyn I was. The cab came ten minutes later. I never spoke a word neither did I say goodbye. I just left.

Throughout the ride to my mother's house, the tears rolled uncontrollably. I wanted to run away and never return to her house, but I had nowhere to go to. The truth was I was afraid to go home so I asked the cab driver to take me to Prospect Park instead. I decided to walk in the park before going home. After two hours, I knew I had to go home.

Do You Hear me Cry?

Can you hear me cry?
When the pain pierces my soul and rattles my bones
Can you hear me cry?
Do you see my tears?
When the odds are against me and all hope is gone
Can you see my tears?
I know why my soul cries.
I now know why my hope died.
I know why my inner child
Like a butterfly that lost its wings
is still trying to fly.
The night growls loudly
The sky shuts its door
Heaven ordered the moon and stars
But in my world they no longer glow.

Can you hear me cry?
Can you see the tears?
I now know why my hope died replaced by my fears.

CHAPTER 4

THE REAL REAL DEAL . . .

My mother sat in the living room waiting. She was furious. She asked me what had happened. I thought she would believe a lie quicker than the truth. So I decided to lie, *a little bit*. I told her the truth up to the point where I drank the alcohol. [**Beginning of Lie**] I told her Sandra and I decided to go to another party because Donna didn't show up. It got too late, and I decided to sleep at Sandra's house. I would have called but I knew she would be mad. I know that was irresponsible of me but I wouldn't do it again. [**End of Lie**]. She believed, and I thought I had gotten over. But that was only the beginning of a life filled with turmoil that was to come.

> I had wanted to tell her the truth about the rape and the hurt, and especially the pain that I felt even as I walked into the house. But I just could not.

I had wanted to tell her the truth about the rape and the hurt, and especially the pain that I felt even as I walked into the house. But I just could not. She had given birth to me and blessed me with life, but she was not the mother I had come expecting. The relationship with her was not what I had expected it to be. She seemed only concerned with her husband and her new baby. I did not matter to her. My role seemed to be that of a live-in helper.

Two weeks later, I found out I was pregnant. My mother suspected it, but I lied the best way I knew how to. Nauseating feelings and dizziness became a part of my

everyday life. I desperately tried to hide it from her, but my weakened eyes deceived me. I never knew being pregnant felt so horrible. Other women made it seem so easy. It was difficult for me to work. So after my mother and her husband left for work, I returned home where I could sleep, because that's all I wanted to do. Simple tasks as just washing the dishes left me very weak.
I wanted to confide in her, and to tell her how I felt, but I could not. As she sat in the sofa across from the kitchen, I knew our conversation occurred for one reason - that she could see whether I was pregnant or not. She had never conversed with me for such a long period before. So I knew she did so because she suspected that I was pregnant. She had asked me about my menstruation for almost a week, but I had lied to her. Thinking back now, she knew before I knew that I was pregnant. I guess mothers can tell.

I eventually went for prenatal care. I was given vitamins and iron tablets, which made me dizzier when I took them. They ended up in the bottom of my bag. I did not fathom having an abortion. I hardly knew what that was anyway. In Jamaica, I was very sheltered. Words like abortion were never in my vocabulary. And anyway, being pregnant meant that I would finally have someone to love and someone to love me back.
After leaving Jamaica emptiness had lingered painfully within, maybe now it would finally die. The love I had come expecting from my mother was not there. She had spent most of her time with her 'new found family'. I now know that I would never have a mother's love that I so desperately desired. It was now obvious that I had given away sure genuine love from my grandparents and

sister for something that never was, and never seemed as though it would ever happen. I had come with hopes of gaining my mother's love that I never got as a child. Instead she offered me a job as a caregiver for a son that would know my mother's love.

The Truth

If I spoke the truth
If my heart revealed its fears
Would you sympathize?
Would you help me hide
From the foes inside
That tortures me to lie?
Help me to reveal
The truth.
Don't just hear, listen.
Listen to the voice of my heart.
If I say the truth
Would you listen.
Please, just listen.

CHAPTER 5
REALITY CHECK

I was awakened by my mother's vulgarity. From the tone of her voice I could tell she had found out that I was pregnant. Fear immediately took a hold of me. I was scared. She was calling me all sorts of names. I lay on the sofa pretending to be asleep, hoping that she would go away. I kept hoping that she would see me sleeping and leave. A deep feeling of fear clutched my inside. She continued calling my name amongst the many other names she labeled me. But I continued to pretend to be asleep.

> "Wake up, get off my sofa!" she yelled. "You are so easy, so cheap, you slut." Standing in the doorway to her bedroom she continued to shout, "and I should have aborted you, I don't know why I didn't abort you!!!" . . . Her words sank deeper than any cut I had endured from Paul's manhood.

"Wake up, get off my sofa!" she yelled. "You are so easy, so cheap, you slut." Standing in the doorway to her bedroom she continued to shout, "and I should have aborted you, I don't know why I didn't abort you!!!!" I could not believe the words. I was numb all over my body. Paul had taken my gift, and that had hurt physically and emotionally. But nothing hurt more than the words she spoke. Her words sank deeper than any cut I possibly had gotten from Paul's manhood.

It felt as though she had just grabbed in and ripped every hope out of my soul from inside me. How could

someone who had *never* been there for me throughout my entire life speak words like she did? I did not understand. I could not understand why she had chosen those words. Maybe that was how she felt all along and now had found a reason to say it.
My life suddenly seemed hopeless.
Ilza had warned me numerous times about coming to America, I just had not listened. She had said our mother never really cared about us, and never would. We were the only two of her children who never knew what it was like to have a mother to love us, not even for a year. And from where I stood in Brooklyn, we never would. I wanted to cry but no tears came, I was too numb. I wanted to scream and run back home to my secure home in Jamaica. I wanted to hear my granddaddy tell me how much he loved me once more, like he did each night before I went to sleep. Instead I heard the words only strangers spoke about their enemies.
A strange emptiness sank deep down inside, which caused me to feel weak and near unconsciousness. Me being pregnant must have been a great disappointment to her or for her. Or maybe it damaged her pride. But, she had been a number in the teenaged-pregnancy statistics too. She had gotten pregnant at sixteen years old with Ilza. I know parents do not want their children to make the same mistake. But she was never a parent to me. I wanted to scream and run back home to Jamaica, but maybe there was no home there for me anymore.
Suddenly all I could see was a worm-filled apple. The words she screamed wishing she had aborted me, rang over and over in my ears. The pain of the hurt overcame any dizziness and nausea I felt.
I had no friends, no family; I did not have Ilza to tell me

it would be okay. I was all alone in the big apple. The thought of God entered my mind, and I quickly rejected it. I did not want to think of God right now, because I had begged him to change her mind as she stood calling me names and telling me to get out, and he had not. She still stood feet away, still insisting that I leave her house immediately.

"Get out of my house, NOW!!" She screamed. "Come on, you're going too slow," she said reaching in the closet that kept my clothes. She grabbed a garbage bag and dumped my clothes in it. Recognizing the sweater and jeans that she had bought, she quickly reached in and pulled them back out, and threw them both on the floor.

"I don't want you back in my house, you're not staying in here and eat my food, you're too easy man, get out!!!!" Her Jamaican accent was more pronounced now. I knew she was at her threshold of anger.

Slowly I put my sneakers on hoping that somewhere, somehow, she would come over and hug me. Somewhere, somehow, God would intervene and change her heart. *Maybe* she would apologize. Maybe I would hear the words 'I did not mean it,' 'I over reacted,' 'how could you?' or maybe she would tell me that everything would be okay and we would see this through together. I secretly hoped that this was all a dream; that I was not here in New York. That I was actually in Jamaica sleeping securely beside my sister on our bed. Hearing my grandfather telling me to go to sleep and that he loved me very much. But I was brought back to reality when my mother opened the door and the sounds of the iron against the floor from the iron bar that served as a security device, made a loud noise. She then beckoned me towards the door to get out.

As I left her house, she slapped my face and slammed her door shut. I did not want to go but I had to. I did not know where I could go, but I had to leave the comfort of her house. All alone in the big apple, no one to tell me that everything would be okay. All I had wanted from my mother was love. Not money. Not clothes. Just love. I had come to America without a green card, but I worked. She told me that it would be 'nice' if I could help to support my two sisters in Jamaica so it would be less strenuous on her financially. And I had wanted to be 'nice' for her to love me, so I bought clothes and shoes and whatever else they needed. So all I wanted was love, unconditional love. A love that withstood all obstacles of life. A mother's pure innocent and unconditional love. But I guess that was asking too much.

As I walked towards the big door that protected the apartment building from the cold winds of November with my garbage bag as my suitcase, I remembered sitting with my mother in the kitchen as she cooked two days before. I remembered her repeatedly telling me how at times in Jamaica she had struggled to find bread and milk for her four children, while Ilza and I were given a pampered life. She said there were times when she did not have milk, and her four children drank Milo without the milk. Maybe she had wanted to see me suffer like she said she did at times in Jamaica. As I stood on the cold street of Brooklyn I fought hard to understand why she had a hateful disposition for me, but I never found the answer.

Where would I go? Who could I call? I would *never* call Paul. I could not fathom living with a man let alone the man that raped me. I could not bear to think of him ever touching me again. I could also have gone to my aunt who lived on the third floor upstairs, but my mother had warned me before I left that if I did she would call Immigration. Was I crazy to keep the baby? If keeping my baby meant I was crazy, I guess I was.

In the brisk November cold, I stood alone and tried to stop several cabs. As though I was transparent, none stopped. With one last hope inside I looked at the window of my mother's apartment and wished that she would see me and call me back in, but that was all just wishful thinking.

Finally a cab stopped. As I entered the cab, I looked at the dark shaded window of her apartment once more. But her lights remained off. I guessed she slept peacefully once again, now that the stranger no longer lived in her apartment.

"Where are you heading to?" The bearded man in the front seat asked.

I had no idea. Jamaica, maybe? I just wanted to go home. Back to the family that I knew. Away from this cold drenched place. Away from the coldness that enveloped my mother, that kept her heart.

Deep within I somehow wished the cab driver to be a serial killer who would put an end to all my misery -- the deep pain that clutched my heart that made my bones ached and my palms wrenched with pain. I was too scared to kill myself, but I would gladly volunteer myself as a lamb for slaughter.

"Can you stop please, at a telephone?" I asked amidst my tears.

"Sure, but is something wrong?" He asked concerned, as he pulled closer to the curb where the phone was.

"That's okay," I answered, stepping out of his car towards the phone. I quickly dialed the number and prayed that someone was there.

The voice on the phone was my aunt's ex-boyfriend, Ronnie. I quickly explained the situation to him and asked if I could stay at his house for a couple of days. I was glad to hear him say yes. Then I asked him if he could pay for the cab because I was broke.

I had met Ronnie in Jamaica at the hospital when my aunt was stabbed by her brother and almost died. Although I was only eleven years old I had a huge crush on my aunt's fiancé as she lay suffering on her bed. Now here I was six to seven years later about to live with him. The crush had gone a long time ago. Now all I could think of was how to survive.

So Familiar

It is true what they say,
A bird in the hand is worth two in the bush.
I gave it all away.
The familiar love, the familiar care, the familiar trust.
Came searching like the dog with the bone
Dropped what I had for a reflection of what I thought was love.
Journeyed just to find
A mother's love -
unconditional.
Instead I found the words
that killed the hope
of my soul.
I found the truth hidden sixteen years
I never should have been
I should have been aborted.
Her words pierce my soul I wished I aborted you."

CHAPTER 6

A WAY OUT OF NOWHERE...

I stayed with Ronnie for the next two weeks. He made sure I was comfortable. He slept on the sofa in his living room and I stayed in his bedroom. I really was not comfortable, but I had no other choice. I was not comfortable because I had never slept in a house with a man other than my grandfather, and more recently when I lived with my mother and her husband, *and* I hated staying there alone whenever he left for work but I knew I had no other choice and knew I had to make the best of it. I really felt as though I was intruding on his privacy. One day after Ronnie left for work my mother called and told me to move back in and I did. My mother found my phone book and had tracked me down. I was like an abused spouse hungering for love. I was glad to go back home. I hated changes. And I thought it love when she asked me to return home. Maybe finally she had started to love me.

But after I returned home, the weeks that followed made me realize that I was only asked back home so I would continue baby-sitting.

Things became uncomfortable again when she found out that I wanted to spend time alone instead of babysitting. I didn't feel like babysitting *every* single day.

Sometimes I just wanted to go window-shopping for the baby. But she wanted me to take my little brother. What would it look like with me pushing a young baby and pregnant at my age? It was humiliating. I tried it before. There were stares and whispers. Who could blame them? And I didn't even have a ring on my finger. Disgraceful!

And to make matters worse she did not even offer me a dollar to babysit.

So she boldly told me if I was not going to baby-sit my brother then there was no place there for me. As much as I wanted to stay I preferred to leave. I felt used. I just couldn't understand why it was so difficult for her to treat me like her child. I decided to leave. Again. I had asked her friend, Debra, if I could stay with her until I found somewhere to go. The truth was I had nowhere to go. And unfortunately her friend was moving to Texas in three days. She was relocating. Just my luck. I was homeless, jobless, and pregnant with no green card. Once again my mother tracked me down because she needed my assistance. And once again like a fool I went back home. I didn't want to and wish I didn't have to but I had nowhere else to go. I was homeless. And she knew I didn't know the system. I could have gotten help, but I didn't know the system. I was a stranger in an unknown land.

The time came and went so quickly. I was seven and a half months pregnant when she tracked me down to return home. Furthermore, I knew the baby would arrive soon. I therefore knew I had to find a place to stay. Her home was the only place I could stay even though it came with a price. I had to baby-sit to pay my way there.
I was due to deliver on June 14. I no longer experienced the nauseous or dizzy feelings. That was the worst time of my life other than hearing my mother said she should have aborted me. I remember the time during my first trimester, kneeling in the bathroom vomiting so hard I thought my kidneys would come through my mouth. I could hear my mother's husband telling her that I sounded sick. I also heard her telling him good for me because that's what I looked for. Looking back she

never bothered to ask how I got pregnant. She only asked who the father was.

I also remember praying to God that the baby was a girl. I wanted a girl to love the way I was never loved. I remember kneeling on the center table in my mother's living room and praying to God. I asked him for a daughter who would love me unconditionally, and who would serve him better than I could ever serve him. I prayed that I would love her unconditionally. I wanted him to teach me the ways of a good mother. I needed his help to avoid the trend of abandoning a child like my mother's mother did to her and like she did to Ilza and me. I wanted to know how to love my daughter the way I had always wanted my mother to love me.

CHAPTER 7

BEGINNING OF LOVE...

My labor pain started at midnight June 13th. I was awoken by mild cramps in my lower abdomen. I woke my mother to tell her about the cramps. Days before she agreed to accompany me to the hospital. She instructed me to take a shower while she called a cab. Throughout the journey to the hospital she kept asking me the level of the pain. I thought it was nothing. She laughed and said that it was not actual labor but just the onset. I was surprised to know she intended on staying with me at the hospital. Maybe seeing me in pain would give her a deeper satisfaction. Because I was positive it wasn't because of love.

> This was indeed the most horrifying experienced I ever had.

The next six hours found me in intense pain. The pain was more than I could bear. My mother stayed with me throughout the entire ordeal. My back felt as though it was being opened with a knife; the pain seemed to last forever. The nurse placed a monitor on my abdomen, which seemed to worsen the pain. This was indeed the most horrifying experience I ever had. I saw the moon, the stars, and the heaven above opened. I reached beyond galaxies unheard of. The pain was frightening almost unto death.

My 'water' still had not broken within the 2 hours that I had been there. The attending doctor came and eventually 'broke it'. He just reached up and then a warm flow of water came after. No explanation, nothing. The pain became even more intense. Thoughts

of not staying alive kept flashing through my mind. The pain was the most excruciating pain I had ever felt. The ordeal seemed to last forever, though it only lasted six hours.
The urge to push finally came. The nurse beckoned me not to push, but it was easier said than done. They wheeled me off to the delivery room. My mother stood close by me. Finally it was all over. Finally it was worth it all. My bundle of joy was finally here. She was beautiful. And her name was Sulei. Somewhere throughout the delivery my mother wept. I wanted to believe she had cried because of my pain. But my hurt wouldn't let me. My heart still ached from her words. It still embraced the coldness that now existed after she kicked me out and after I realized that all I will ever be to her is her son's baby-sitter. My heart led me to believe her tears were tears of sadness that her mother had not been there for her when she had her first child. I knew her tears were not for me. Not with the bitterness she felt for this stranger in her house.

My prayers were answered on June 14th. I had a baby girl, who weighed seven pounds fourteen ounces. She was my pride and joy. She was wrinkled and beautiful. Although she looked everything like Paul I loved her. Looking at her I knew I had forgiven Paul. Nothing he did mattered anymore. Maybe I felt that way because I had yearned for love. And now it was finally here. Maybe I was stupid to keep my baby due to the circumstance of conception. But that didn't matter, because I desperately wanted my baby to love.
My mother visited me every day in the hospital. Whatever she cooked for dinner she brought a portion for me. I had a temperature so I had to stay in bed.

Although I had a normal delivery I received twenty-seven stitches. The nurse said that was because I pushed when they told me not to. It was difficult to walk. I walked with my legs wide open, just like a duck.

The day was finally here for me to go home. My mother and her husband came to get us. My little brother was still at his godmother's house. On our way home we stopped to get him. I missed him terribly. I loved him with all my heart. As he walked out the house his eyes searched the inside of the car. A smile formed across his lips when he saw me. As he neared the car his eyes moved from my eyes to my hands that held the baby. He gave her the nastiest look I ever saw and then rolled his eyes as if to say, "yeah, I don't know where *you* think you're going, but I sure know it *ain't* in my house." I knew he would have a difficult time seeing another baby in the house because he now had to share the attention with someone else.

We were finally home. The ride home was painful. As I walked up the stairs my mother joked that I walked like a duck. It was difficult walking up the stairs, but I was glad to be home again. It was finally over. I could breathe again.

My obstetrician had arranged for a visiting nurse to assist with the baby. She came at 9 o'clock every morning for two weeks. She made sure Sulei was fed, bathed and cared for. She took my temperature every day to make sure I was okay. She taught me how to give Sulei a sponge bath because her umbilical cord was still attached. Water was not allowed near it. I was afraid of caring for her while it was attached. The day it fell off I was happy. I could now hold her without being afraid of hurting her.

CHAPTER 8
THE CALL . . .

"**W**ake up, it's a Detective Jones," my mother had a worried look on her face.
"Hello," I answered curiously still somewhat asleep.
"Is this Karlei?" The voice on the other end asked firmly. His voice sounding high pitched.
"Yes."
"This is Det. Jones. Do you know a Paul Sample?"
"Yes, he's my daughter's father."
It sounded strange saying 'my daughter's father'. I should have said, 'yes, he's a rapist'. But it really didn't matter because I now had the greatest gift of all. And why did he have a detective calling my house?
"He's in Kings County Hospital, he was shot tonight."
My mother was standing there quietly. I guess she must have noticed the change in my expression because she kept asking me what was wrong beneath her breath, with her eyebrows arched.
"Is he seriously hurt, how many times was he shot?"
"Ma'am I don't know, he just asked me to call you. You can call Kings County in the morning and find out everything you need to know."
"Okay, thank you." But before I could place the receiver back on the handset my mother started questioning me.
"What is it?" My mother asked curiously again.
"Paul was shot and is in the hospital," trying to sound as calm as possible.
After all, my mother still had no idea I was raped. She had called me easy and cheap. And maybe I was. Maybe I deserved to be raped. Maybe I had called it on myself by not insisting to leave his apartment. I was too ashamed to even admit to her that I was raped. I can just imagine what she would say. Maybe she wouldn't even

believe. Like the time she sent me to Key Food when we lived on Washington Avenue. Three aged men in a car followed me down the block of Montgomery between Washington Avenue and Bedford. When I finally arrived, she asked me what took me so long to return home. When I explained to her that the men in the car followed me and to avoid them I went back to the supermarket as I knew they could not turn the car around as Montgomery was a one-way street coming home. She had given me a look of disbelief. So now, why would I tell her I was raped?
"Is he dead, is he going to be okay?" She continued.
"I don't know, the detective said he did not know much, that I should call in the morning at Kings County Hospital."
"Oh, okay. In the morning then," she said walking back to her room.
I was glad to be alone. I had wanted her to leave immediately. As I walked back to my room, the tears flowed uncontrollably. They felt warm against my cheeks. Why was I crying after what he had done to me? It shouldn't matter. But for some strange reason it did. Maybe I had wanted a life different for Sulei than I had as a child. Despite the manner in which I conceived her, I loved her. I wanted her regardless of how she came. I also had wanted Paul to somehow be a part of her life regardless of what he did. Or maybe I cried because I brought her into this confusion. But I couldn't have done anything else other than having her because I knew she was a gift from God. And after seeing Sulei nothing matter anymore.
As I lay on the bed I looked across to where she slept. How could they have done this to her? He hadn't even seen her yet. But suddenly I became confused because I

really had not intended for him to see her. I cried until my throat hurt. I cried because I never envisioned this for my first child. I never envisioned this for any child of mine. I wanted the perfect family. The white picket fence. The car in the driveway. I wanted it all.
I picked her up and held her close to my breast though she still lay sleeping. I wished that she was big enough to fill my arms. Maybe then I could hug her hard enough to squeeze the hurt from within me, a pain whose existence I didn't understand. The more I held her, the more the tears flowed. They dripped softly in her hair. As I held her tiny frame within my arms, I spoke softly into her ear that everything would be alright, as if somehow she understood my words.

"Karlei, get up it's the phone," my mother was standing over me with her arms outstretched with the phone. Morning had come so quickly. I must have fallen asleep between tears. Propping up as quickly as I could, I nervously placed the receiver to my ear, and quickly glanced towards the window. Morning really had come too soon.
"Hello, Karlei," it was Paul's nephew, Laten.
"Hi, Laten. How is he?" I asked hastily before giving him a chance to tell me what really happened or letting him know that I knew.
"Oh you heard. Dem shot Paul," >>> [**Paul was shot**] his Jamaican accent blended in with his Brooklyn accent.
"Yes, I heard, the detective called me last night and told me. Is he badly wounded?"
"The boys them shot him nine times. Is two of them came with guns I heard." His voice was filled with pain. It was difficult for him to speak. His voice quivered over the phone. I didn't understood why now they were

calling. What did I care? Why should I care? But I couldn't blame Laten for calling because he too did not know. He did not know how I conceived. He knew many things his uncle did, but this was not one of them.
Laten promised to call back after he went to see his uncle. He told me to stay home with Sulei and wait for his call. Paul had several nephews but Laten was his favorite. I had spoken to him twice before I was raped. Laten called back twenty minutes later. His voice still sounded weak, but not as before.
"Him may be left paralyzed. They had to tear his clothes off him."
I could tell that Laten was in a lot of pain and so was I. I was in a lot of pain I did not understand. Or maybe I did. I knew my baby's future had started out all wrong. But I chose to not take life away from her because I had not given her life . . . God had! Maybe it was post-partum depression that caused my unexplained pain, or maybe it was the pain I felt knowing the familiar road of not having a father beside me. My whole body felt weak. I hadn't heard my mother telling me she had to leave for work and that she would call me as soon as she reached her job. I was glad to be left alone. The pain was too much.
"Do you guys know who did it?" I asked as if it made a difference.
"Yes, I think I know who it was, but I'm not sure."
I could tell his pain was deep. After we said bye I finally let it all out. I was alone now and could release the pain. My pain came pouring out like rain amidst the tears that showered my pillow.

As the Night Lay in the Dark

It was like an owl's voice; A soft small echo
In the darkness of the forest; Too thick to find a willow
Flying or perched
Too dark to see the light
Peering through the tree's branch
Like the pain within my heart
The stillness of the owl's whisper
Echoes in the darkness that thickens the night
Against the trees
That lined the paths winding to and fro
Leading to where no one knows
It's a panging pain, a lasting pain
A pain that lingers and send shivers
It's a dirty pain
A pain that last and last
And digs deeper and deeper
Between the muscles and in the bones
And carries on and on
It's like the night that lay in the dark
Still
The night that releases all sounds
The night that harbors silence
The night that has boundaries
The night that lay in the darkness
The pain that lay within

CHAPTER 9

REHAB . . .

Laten called me very often. Laten kept me informed as to how long Paul would stay in the hospital.

Paul stayed in the hospital for thirteen months. After three months in the Med-Surgical Unit he was transferred to the Rehabilitation Center. I took Sulei to visit him on several occasions. I was not sure if I took her to visit him as a father or to see him suffer. He was never the same. He still had his personality, but he kept reflecting back to the day it all happened.
Two men armed with 45mm automatic handguns 'came for him' he said. They fired all eighteen rounds at him. Fortunately only nine penetrated his body. I always viewed the nine shots as one for each month I was pregnant.

My father was killed with just one gunshot to his head. And here he was nine shots and still alive. He underwent several surgeries. He now had a colostomy. His intestine was damaged. The doctors weren't sure if he would ever walk again. He refused to accept that fact and was determined to start therapy. He was convinced that he would walk again – one day.
Laten stood by Paul throughout the entire ordeal. Laten and I were both the same age but he was more mature than I was and much more streetwise than I would ever be. His girlfriend Shelly was a true essence of fashion. She tailored herself in all the finest clothing. She wore Gucci boots with matching pocket book. She was truly elegant in even the simplest of clothing. She was the total opposite of who I was. And though she was about seven months pregnant she glowed. Secretly I envied

her and her flare. But I knew no matter how hard I tried I would never have that look. I just didn't have that flair. Life at home became unbearable because my mother insisted on me staying home and babysitting. She insisted that I forget about Paul. I couldn't. She wanted me to forget about Paul not because he raped me and not because she cared. She wanted me to forget about Paul so I could focus on babysitting. I rebelled knowing her motive. I was not sure why I even took Sulei to visit him. Maybe because Laten had begged me to or maybe I wanted Sulei to know her father despite the circumstances. Or maybe I went because my mother wanted me not to. My mother was only satisfied with me when I babysat. And once again my whole life seemed to go downhill. I was never accepted as her daughter, only as a babysitter. Once again it became obvious.

Paul was finally discharged from the hospital. Laten got an apartment so he could share it with Paul. Shelly decided to move in with Laten. I visited Paul as often as was practical. I enjoyed seeing Sulei interact with her father. My mother and I went to war again. We fought hard this time. Every room was like a minefield. The wrong step and an explosion occurred. She told me I had to move. Again. She told me it was best that I moved in with Paul to help care for him. She couldn't accept the fact that I could not babysit my brother every single day. Furthermore, all she was giving was room and shelter. Paul's nephew Laten gave me money for Sulei. My mother was not satisfied that it was not practical for an eighteen year old to baby sit two babies every single day. My brother was still a baby, he was only a year older than Sulei.

My heart was ripped to shreds because she was serious that she wanted me out. I had nowhere to go once again. Eventually I begged Laten and Shelly to stay at the apartment.
Living with my rapist! How about that?

I wanted to tell my mother that Paul had raped me but would she even care?

It wasn't difficult living with Paul even though he had lost the ability to ever rape me again. As he sat in his chair he begged me not to tell Laten or anyone that he had lost the ability to function as a man. His secret was very safe with me.
As the months passed I realized living at Paul's house was more hectic than I had imagined. He had a colostomy bag on the left side of his stomach, and was unable to care for it. At first it disgusted me but I conditioned my mind to the extent that it no longer bothered me. The smell of the colostomy made me nauseous at times. Removing it was the most gruesome chore ever. But I did it anyway. Sulei was with her father, something I never had.

Laten and Shelly fought constantly. I never understood why. As pregnant as she was, they fought like cats. She would scratch him. He would take whatever he could find to throw at her. They fought day and night. It became unbearable. I told myself I held on for Sulei's sake, a home, a father. Even though to me he was a rapist, to her he was her father. I held on because I wanted her to be with her father and we had nowhere to go.

Shelly enjoyed partying even though she was pregnant. I was the total opposite of Shelly. I enjoyed staying home. Laten questioned why Shelly could not stay home like I did. Shelly and I had few things in common. Shelly and Paul were more compatible and Laten and I seemed more compatible.

Growing up in Jamaica, my grandfather was extremely strict. My routine was school, home, home, and school. Staying home was a part of me, while partying was a part of Shelly. And that created conflict in their home. As the months passed, the tension grew stronger. The relationship between Shelly and me became tense. The relationship between Laten and me also became uneasy. There was hardly any relationship between Laten and Shelly any more. I kept losing weight. I was at my thinnest. Eventually I called my mother to ask her to go back home, but she said no. I had conditioned my mind that if she allowed me to come back home I would just be her live in babysitter. I was losing it mentally and knew I had to get out.
Laten started having an affair with a girl that lived a block away from where he worked. He had confided in Paul and Paul confided in me. Paul had also confided that Laten sold drugs and so did he. Now it all made sense. The money. The clothes. The Gucci bag and boots. The free spending. It all made sense. I didn't believe him at first. But after he took me in Laten's room and showed me what he said was cocaine, I had no other choice but to believe. I had been so stupid and naive. That very minute I knew I had to get out. Maybe if Shelly knew she too would leave. I decided to confide in Shelly and decided to tell her everything I knew. Shelly told Laten everything I told her that Paul said that

Laten said and did. All hell broke loose. Everyone but Shelly and myself denied everything, which made me look like a liar. I was placed on the most hated list. And the worst part of it? Shelly already knew they sold drugs.

I knew I had to get out. I told Paul I couldn't take it anymore. He asked me who would take care of him. He swore to remove my ability to walk should I try to leave. I was the only help he had and he refused to give it up. He also refused to allow me to take Sulei. But I knew I had to leave. I had to somehow draft a plan because I had to get out. But I knew I had to do it when he was not at home. I didn't have anywhere to go but I had to get out. I decided to leave whenever he went to one of his therapy sessions at the hospital's outpatient clinic with Laten. After washing our clothes, I would leave them in the laundry bag making it easier to pack my clothes and Sulei's. But I had nowhere to go. That was my main concern. I had *nowhere* to go. I had no one to turn to. But I knew I had to get out. As much as I had wanted Sulei to grow with a father beside her I could no longer stay. It was just too much. I was only nineteen years old, caring for a baby and a man in a wheelchair who wasn't even my man. Who had taken the only gift I could have possibly given to my husband. But I had forgiven him because in return I received a gift that taught me love and gave me strength and inner peace. I had lied to myself that I had forgiven him because it was the only place I had to stay and no one knew he raped me. I was ashamed of what I had become – a far cry than who my grandfather raised me to be . . . But now it was too much responsibility. I had to get out. I decided to get out when he was not around.

Captivity

Bob Marley said,
"No woman, no cry"
But the pain is just too real
Marley said,
"Dry the tears from your eyes"
But yow . . . this was the real deal
I was held captive
By my confusion
Should I go?
Should I stay?
Should I remain THE victim?
Peter Tosh once sang
"If your first love have broke your heart
There's something can be done
Don't have your faith in love
Remembering what's been gone"
Not a first love
Just a first hurt
Not a broken heart
Just a stolen gold
I wanted to keep for my husband
But it was stolen
From the rapist thief
No one would understand
Why I did what I did
I don't even understand
The life that I chose to live
It doesn't make sense
It doesn't all add up
My confusion led me into the wilderness
To find shelter within no-man's home . . .

CHAPTER 10

THE ESCAPE...

T hat weekend after I went to the Laundromat I kept our clothes in the bag as I had planned, removing only his clothes. I was glad to know the only thing he suspected me of doing was becoming lazy as he and Laten often joked.

The day for our escape was finally here. Laten had just drove off to take Paul for therapy. I made sure they were gone by standing outside pretending to help Laten put Paul in the car. As soon I was convinced that they were gone I ran back in the house. Hurriedly, I packed my clothes and then called a cab, which took forever to come. Or so it seemed. I was afraid that they would return home for something that Laten forgot to take with them as he sometimes does.

Sulei slept through my entire plan and for that I was extremely thankful, as she would definitely had slowed me down. I took all my clothes out of the house in black garbage bags and placed them on the sidewalk in front of the house. Black garbage bags held everything I owned. My heart pounded twice than its normal pace against my now thin body frame. Every five minutes I went to see if the cab came, but was always disappointed. It took forever to come. I decided to go back in for Sulei and held her in my arms, so when the cab came, if it ever did, we could just leave. I became very scared because I knew if Paul saw me trying to leave, he might try to hurt me as he had promised to do on many occasions.

I quickly went back into the house for Sulei. Walking back outside, I made sure all the locks on the door were secured. The cab was still not there when I returned. From where I stood I could hear the sound of a car coming. My throat tightened and my heart palpitated. My eyes bulged as the car came closer. It was the cab. Finally. As I walked towards the oncoming car, Laten's

car swerved the corner. Oh hell! Busted! I quickly jumped in the car. Laten increased his speed and jumped out of his car and began approaching the cab.
"Please go!!!" I begged the cab driver.
"Wait!" Laten shouted to the cab driver.
"No, drive, drive, please drive!!!" As I checked the locks on the door to make sure they were locked. I was even more afraid now than I thought I would be.
"What?" The driver asked. I could tell from his accent he was from Africa. "What did you say?" he repeated.
"Just go!!!!!" I screamed.
But the cab still stood there. He could not understand what I was saying. Frustration immediately grabbed a hold of my organs inside.
"Can you please just go! Drive! Please! Just go! Please!"
Laten was an inch away when the cab sped off. I have yet to know which word I used that he understood. But I was glad he did. Sulei became hysterical. She continuously screamed and hollered. Calming her down, I glanced back. Laten was standing in the middle of the street. I had come so close. So close. Too close. I would never go back. Just then I realized that I had left all my clothes on the pavement in front of the house. My clothes. I had left my clothes. I had left everything. They were on the sidewalk in front of the apartment. Sulei's pictures, all her pictures were in the bags. Her baby brag book that I kept her milestones of accomplishments, that too was in the bag, and so were our clothes, all of our clothes. All we had left was the clothes on our bodies and the shoes on our feet. I had to go back. I had to take the chance. I just had to go back.
"Can you please take me back?" I nervously asked the driver.
"Go back?" he asked as he glanced at me in his mirror as if I was crazy.

Now he understood me? After all that? Now he understood me? I was too caught up in the moment to even query why he understood now but didn't when my life and Sulei's was in jeopardy.

"Yes. Please." After answering him I too thought I must have been crazy to go back. But I had to. Everything we owned was in the black garbage bags.

"Yes, my clothes. I left it on the pavement in front of the house," I paused then continued to beg, "Please."

He spun the car around, making a screeching noise in the middle of the road and headed back towards the house. Whether he understood everything I said or just a part of it, he was taking me back.

Slowly he turned the corner. Laten's car was no longer there. God was truly good. As he pulled up to the curb, it was clear to see the bags weren't there either. Laten must have put them inside the house. I carefully opened the door and moved swiftly around the house to check for my bags. I had wanted to ask the driver to honk me if anyone came, but I knew it would take forever explaining it to him. My bags were nowhere to be seen. Rushing out the house I prayed to God that I would not encounter Laten or Paul again. As I made my way to the car my eyes were distended with tears. How could this be? Who could have taken them? As I searched for answers I was not so sure if I had even seen them the first time I got in the cab. My mind was too shattered for me to remember. I did not know anything anymore. Everything we owned was totally lost. Gone.

As the car made its way to the end of the block, I decided to call Sulei's godmother, Cherlie, to ask if we could rest there for a night or two. Thereafter I did not know just where we would go.

"Can you please stop?" I asked the cab driver, already placing my hand on the door knob to get out.

I could hear disgust in his voice as he mumbled

something in his native language. I quickly dialed Cherlie's number. She took forever to answer.
"Hello," the voice cracked on the other end of the phone. Cherlie always sounded asleep whenever she answered her phone, even at four in the evening.
"Hello, Cherlie. Can Sulei and I come and stay for two days?" I had no time to procrastinate or pretend. I still was afraid of Paul seeing me. I was still just a couple of blocks away from his house.
"Sure, what happen to you and Paul?"
"I'll tell you when I reach, Cherlie," I replied somewhat frustrated. I was relieved that she did not detect it in my voice or she chose not to comment about it.
She still managed, however, to slip in one of her usual sounds of sarcasm. The truth was I wish I did not have to go there but I had no other choice. I hated inconveniencing anyone and further more I felt like an intruder.

As the car swerved down the busy Nostrand Avenue, crossing over Eastern Parkway my mind shifted to my life back in Jamaica. Never would I have imagined my life spiraling out of control like it was about to. I was use to such a simple life. In Jamaica I lived with my grandparents. In Jamaica I shared love with my sister. In Jamaica I yearned to be with my mother. I gambled everything I had in Jamaica just to be here with my mother. I gambled and lost. Ever since I left Jamaica, my sense of stability had slowly vanished. As I had walked away from the phone and headed towards the cab, I knew my life had definitely changed. Here I was moving again. Here I was homeless again. Two steps forward, eleven steps back. I knew I didn't love Paul, not after he had raped me. But Paul's house was all we ever had.

As the cab headed towards Cherlie's house, I reflected on the past year how my life had totally changed. Never had I imagined that I would end up as a statistic – pregnant teen, high school dropout, and homeless. Now I was. Nineteen years of age and already my life had gone off course. Sitting in the cab in front of Cherlie's home, I inhaled deeply and gathered the courage to face Cherlie's hour-long lecture. But I preferred that to Laten's wrath.

Cherlie lived with her son, Patterson. His father had remarried a 'white lady' as Cherlie referred to her. His father had given Cherlie full custody of Patterson. I admired her strength as a single parent. Never had I imagined that being a mother would have been so difficult. From the outside looking in things seemed pretty easy. But never had I imagined being a teenaged parent was this chaotic. This was real. Unlike the baby dolls I had at home, this was the total opposite. Never before had I fathom that I would constantly have the responsibility of caring for a child. I was not able to throw her aside whenever I became tired of 'playing' with her as I did with my dolls. In the 'real' world it is called 'abuse'. I also came to realize that I could not shake the urine out of her as I did my doll whenever she was fed with water. Or use any old piece of cloth for her diaper as I did my doll just before giving her the water. And I could not use the cloth over and over again like I did the doll. Having a baby cost money. Diapers. Formula. Soap. It all added up. This was real. This was all too real.

I had wanted a baby to love desperately. But never before had I visualized the permanence of the responsibility of having a child. Here I was faced with the reality of adulthood. Live or die. And I chose to live despite the fact my mother wished I hadn't been. I knew

deep within me it was not going to be easy. There had been days when I just wanted to give up. Just disappear. But I could not. Somehow inside, I knew I could not. I could not let my hope collapse.
I have yet to know whatever it was that kept me going. Maybe it was my will to prove to everyone that I would make it. Or maybe I did not collapse simply because someone else depended on my strength. Someone who depended on me not only for the daily necessities of life but depended on me to instill life that was due to her now that she was in this world.
So I chose to live.
I made my way up the windy staircase that led to Cherlie's apartment. She had been looking through her window in anticipation of our coming. She adored Sulei. But I could not help but feel intrusive.
"Come here Sulie," she was always mispronouncing Sulei's name. "Why must your mother move you around so much?" She then continued, "So what happen to you and Paul?" She asked as she continued to play with Sulei, not removing her attention from her for a second. Not even Cherlie knew that I was raped. I was just too ashamed to let anyone know.
"I can't take it anymore," I said shaking my head from side to side in frustration then continuing, "Laten and Shelly were fighting too much and things were not the same. Paul had told me Laten was seeing another girl and I had told Shelly and Shelly went back and told Laten. Laten and Paul lied and said it was not true and Paul told Shelly he did not tell me anything. So eventually I looked like I had made the whole thing up. I really did not know she would say anything back to Laten. Me and my big mouth," I said gasping for air while fidgeting with my braids that hung on my shoulder. Shelly's cousin Erica had nicely braided my hair. But that was before the big confusion happened.

"So why Paul lied?" finally taking her eyes off Sulei for a split second, she glanced confusingly at me.
"Well, he said he did not have any where to go. And it seemed as if I wanted Laten to put him out on the street. I really did not think Shelly would have said anything," pausing from frustration of having to relive the whole ordeal again I continued, "Do you think I would intentionally jeopardize Sulei from having a home?" I asked as I turned to face her fully. I had been sitting not facing her all this time but actually turning towards her direction whenever we spoke.
"Well I hope not, at least for Sulei's sake. I hope not. Because you cannot have this child moving from one place to another," pausing briefly before she continued her lecture. "So did you call your mother?" She asked as she reached for the bottle of juice on her table for Sulei.
"Yes."
"What is she saying-is she letting you come home?"
"No. I asked her, but she said she did not have enough space for Sulei and me. She said if I didn't have Sulei it would have been okay. But her place was a bit small and there was not enough space."
"Not enough space?" she asked laughing, "Your mother's apartment is way bigger than mine, what she mean not enough space? What did you do to your mother Karlei, why she treats you in this manner?"
"Nothing. I did her nothing," I replied as honest as I knew how to be. I had asked myself that question many times before and still did not have an answer. Just what *did* I do to my mother why she hated me?
"Are you sure?" She asked doubtfully.
"Yes I'm sure," I replied.
"That seems hard to believe," she added.
It was hard to believe. But it was the truth. I had done nothing wrong but she somehow did not like me. At least her actions showed me that. I perceived that. It

still hurt inside whenever I remembered her words of how she should have aborted me. It must have rung in my ears a million times or more, the words she told me that night she found out that I was pregnant - "I should have aborted you." I should never have been. It was just luck that got me here in this world and not want. Not wanting me to be, as I had wanted Sulei to be. Pure luck. Luck that maybe then in Jamaica abortion was not prevalent -that kind of luck. Luck that she never could afford an abortion or maybe was too scared to have one - That kind of luck. I was just a lucky, now damaged product that somehow mistakenly made it.

I wanted to finally be able to say to Sulei that it was not my fault or intentions for us to be moving so much. But I couldn't, because the words would not be true, because eventually we would have to move again. I knew I could not stay for too long with Cherlie. There simply was not enough space for Sulei and me. I knew I had to find somewhere to go, and soon. There was nothing more I wanted for Sulei than a stable home. But my life was just one big mistake after another. And from the outlook of things, I doubt it would ever be anything more than that – one big mistake. I remained quiet throughout Cherie's 'sessions' of advice. I answered questions, but volunteered no further information. I was simply just hurting too much.

Six months had passed since Sulei and I first came to stay at Cherlie's house. Sulei had gotten very thin because I did not know how to properly care for a child. She was now one year old and no longer drank formula. She drank milk. At one year old she could not eat anything solid. This was the most trying time as a mother because I did not know what to feed her. The baby food in the jar was very expensive to buy especially because I did not have any money. Furthermore I was just not educated in the childcare division. I soon realized that I had bitten off much more than I could chew to have a baby. But I knew I had to keep focused and determined. I knew I had to keep strong for the both of us. We still did not have any clothes. I borrowed clothes from Cherlie and she bought three outfits for Sulei. I knew Sulei and I needed clothes but I had no money. The days were depressing. After Cherlie left for work and her son left for school, I had the house to myself. With no one around, I became depressed. My life had taken a turn for the worst. Now I knew why Ilza chose to stay in Jamaica. Maybe I should have stayed also. I had to do something. Go somewhere. I couldn't stay another day in the house.

In the mornings after Cherlie left for work I packed a bag with Sulei's diapers and several bottles of milk to take with us on the road. We were going shopping - window shopping. I decided to take a trip to the Queens Center Mall. I did not even have money for the subway, but I decided to go anyway.

As I made my way to the subway my heart pounded with fear that I would be caught trying to get on the train without paying. But I was determined to go anyway. As I entered the subway I searched the entire station to see if a cop was around. I saw none. I firmly held Sulei's hand and made my way through the exit gate.

"Excuse me miss, you did not pay your fare," the tollbooth clerk hollered through the glass.

"Miss, you did not pay your fare!" He continued to yell. I somehow wished he would just shut up. But he continued. And as I vanished down the stairs I could still hear him yelling. As soon as I made my way down the stairs the train came. It was empty. An older lady sat across from us. She admired Sulei throughout the entire travel. She kept counting her money, of which were mostly pennies. Looking at her I wished I had even what she had --- mostly pennies. I did not even have one penny in my pocket. Before leaving I ate a sandwich because I knew I couldn't afford lunch.

The next stop was ours so I slowly got up and carefully held onto the rails. I hated the swerving and the jerking that the train made as it made its way to each stop. Then it would suddenly come to a halt and shove our bodies forward then backward.

The Beginning of Learning to Survive

CHAPTER 11

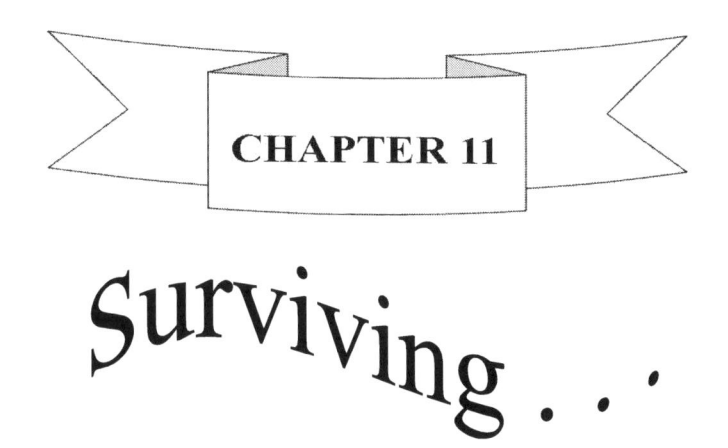

Surviving...
The Beginning

As I walked towards the mall, I searched for its entrance. Sulei felt heavier than usual, or maybe it was because I held her in my arms too long. The 'Don't Walk' sign had already begun flashing when I finally made it across the street. Walking slowly, I shopped with my eyes. That was all I could do. I was broke. It bothered me terribly that I could not adequately provide for my daughter as a mother should. There were so many things that I saw and wanted to buy for her, but I did not even have a dollar.

The weather had changed and she still did not have an appropriate snowsuit. My mother had given us a jacket that my brother outgrew. With the baseball logo on the left side of the sleeve it wasn't hard to tell it belonged to a boy. But I was too glad to have a jacket for her to wear. Any jacket would have been fine. But now as we walked amidst the shoppers in the mall, the guilt of not being able to provide for her grabbed my heart. I knew my mother could have bought her a jacket, but for whatever reason she chose not to. Instead she had given us a worn out jacket that my brother no longer needed. At that moment, I was grateful.

Marcy's was huge. I had never been in the store before. As we stood by the entrance the department store seemed like a giant to us. Then again, we were tiny particles in a big world. We were like atoms, unseen to the naked eye; only that atoms were important, we weren't. Whether we were being compared to Marcy's or to life itself. We were no one. After I left Jamaica, I became no one. And now, I was even more 'a nobody'. I had nothing. I had no money. No clothes. No shoes. Nothing. No family it seemed.

I decided that my first stop would be the kids' department. As I searched through the rack I admired the 'Osh Kosh' and "London Fog' snowsuits. But I resented their price, which started at $69.00. That was a lot. It seemed like an asking price of a million dollars. Sulei needed a snow suit but I knew I couldn't afford any.

The shoe department carried very dainty-looking shoes for small feet. Picking them up and admiring them, I somehow began feeling sorry for myself, but mostly for Sulei. The other children who walked around the store looked properly cared for. Their mothers walked around with signs of prosperity – well done hairstyles, properly dressed, and numerous shopping bags. Although I was broke I decided to take some clothes and try them on Sulei in the fitting room even though I did not intend to buy. I just wanted to 'fit in' with the crowd who mostly strolled around with clothing on their arms. I headed for the fitting room with six sets of clothes and two pairs of shoes.

No one but Sulei and me was in the fitting room. "Hello, Hello?" I shouted as I entered, but no one answered back, just my echo. Slowly, I entered the fitting room, bellowing hello once more. But still no one answered, just the hallow sound of my voice echoing back at me. Once inside I began removing her clothes and fitted one suit at a time. She looked splendid! I could not believe she was my daughter. The shoes fitted her perfectly and the clothes brought such a change in her appearance. I was more excited than she was.

"Don't move Sulei, okay?" I whispered in her ear as I watched her admired herself in the mirror then I quickly walked back to the children's area. The snowsuits still hung on the rack where I had left them. I picked out a pink and white snowsuit and checked the size. It was the perfect fit. Returning to the fitting room I called out once more checking to see if we were still alone. But again no one responded to my yells of hello.

I had tried the last set on her. "Okay Sulei let's take these off," but she resisted.

She did not intend to take them off. Immediately she started to scream as loud as her vocal chords would allow her to. I became frustrated, so I decided to let her wear them. The truth was I did not want to take them off either. Had I wanted to, there was no way on Earth that I would have allowed her to keep them on. But I could not leave the store without the clothes she had on and the others on the floor. I was petrified. How could I possibly walk out the store with security at the door? I decided that I would, no matter what.

Returning to the fitting room I emptied everything out of the pink Jansport backpack that I carried and replaced them with the other suits of clothing that were still scattered on the floor. I then carefully covered the clothing with Sulei's diapers and bottles of milk. I then stuffed the jacket I had gotten from my mother in the corner of the room and fitted on her new snowsuit. She looked gorgeous, but I was too scared to really admire her. I was afraid of leaving the store without paying for the merchandise. I was *very* scared. As I walked out of the dressing room I picked up the teddy bear she had played with since we came in the store. We then walked as normal as we could towards the exit sign on the first floor.

Once outside the mall, I could not believe what I had done. I was still shaking all over. I was definitely afraid. As I walked to the subway, my feet felt like running instead. Ironically, I thanked the Lord.

The ride home seemed much quicker than our trip to the mall. I began to feel somewhat bothered that I would have to lie to Cherlie. I knew the minute we walked in she would comment on Sulei's new clothes and shoes. What would I tell her? I knew I would have to lie. But what would I say?

Sulei had fallen asleep in my arms. I was comforted to know that she was warm. The jacket my mother gave her was warm but without a doubt I was sure that she was warmer in her new snowsuit.

The walk home was more tedious because I had to carry her as she lay lifeless in my arms, because she was still asleep. Finally we were home. Patterson was on his way back from the supermarket just as we reached the door. Perfect timing. He did not speak much. He always kept to himself. Sulei and I shared his room with him. He had a twin bed and a day bed in his room. We slept on his day bed that was alongside one of the walls in his room. He had a fish tank with the most beautiful tropical fish I had ever seen. He also had a parakeet. He allowed his parakeet to fly around the room most of the time. I dreaded the parakeet's playtime and was always overjoyed when he was put back in his cage. I always felt our stay would have been perfect without the bird. But that was the bird's home, and not ours.

Once inside the apartment I realized Cherlie was not home as yet. I was thankful because I had more time to think of a lie to tell her where Sulei's new clothes came from. As I passed the kitchen and headed for Patterson's room I glanced at the pot on the stove. I could tell that she had cooked. Cooking was one of Cherlie's favorite tasks, next was cleaning. Her house was always immaculately kept. Her cooking was exceptionally tasteful. And her menus were extravagant. Her 'tamale pie' was my favorite. She made it from ground beef with a touch of spiciness. She was a superb cook. I was tempted to look in the pot, but I refrained from doing so. I was hungry, but I decided to wait until she came home. I must have fallen asleep, because when I awoke all the lights were off but Cherlie sat alone in the kitchen.

"Hi sleeping beauty, boy you sleep dead. Do you know how long I was trying to wake you up and you would not budge," she said softly as she stirred the pot slowly. I was exhausted from all the walking I had done at the mall earlier.

Slightly smiling I peeked at the space between the curtains at the window. The sun had gone down. The brightness of the day was gradually fading. Now that Fall was here the glare of the sun in the kitchen retreated earlier than normal. The daytime seemed shorter and the nights got colder, sooner.

"Did you hear me?" her voice superficially pitched higher.

"No, what did you say?" I really had not heard anything that she had said. My mind had drifted off to Jamaica. I wondered what Ilza was doing right at this moment. I missed her so much. Never would she imagined everything that I had gone through for the past two years. Everything had gone wrong. Everything. I was the total opposite of the character in that fairy tale book whose touch turned everything into gold. Everything I touched disintegrated. I was a total failure. But deep within I knew someday, one day, for Sulei's sake I would make it somehow. I owed it to her.

"Karlei, what is wrong with you?" Cherlie must have been calling me several times before I heard her because her voice was filled with frustration.

"Nothing, just thinking of my sister back home," I said trying to shrug off the tears that had formed in my eyes.

"You miss them?" she asked caringly.

"Very much," I wish my pride had not hindered me from allowing the hurt to escape from my body – the hurt that was penned up on the inside like an ambushed animal in its trap. I wanted to let it all out. But I could not. I wanted to have a good cry but I could not. I never allowed anyone to see my tears or my pain. I never allowed anyone to know how much I could be hurt.

Cherlie's voice broke my meditation, "Guess who I saw

today?" She announced with excitement filling her voice.

Shrugging my shoulders I mumbled that I couldn't guess.

"Your cousin Peter."

"I have a cousin Peter?" I asked. My family was so big and separated I wondered how he came to be my cousin, if in fact he was.

"Your father's cousin. They call him Pete."

"Okay. Now I know who he is. I had met him a long time ago shortly after I came from Jamaica. He owns two houses somewhere here in Brooklyn, right?"

"Yes. I saw him today. I told him you were here staying with me and he said you should come to visit him."

"Where does he live?"

As her eyes circled the ceiling as if the answer hung there, she finally answered. "Somewhere off Madison Ave."

"Oh," I replied as if I knew exactly where it was.

"We'll go tomorrow."

I had heard of Pete. He had two grocery stores. He had been in the USA since the age of five. He invested his money wisely and now it really paid off. Suddenly my hunger left. The thought of moving Sulei into another home took its toll on my mind. Just when she had gotten familiar with the house as her home, we had to leave again. Would I ever be able to give her stability? From the look of my life and the path it was taking, I doubted it very much. I knew that I would have to leave Cherlie's house eventually, but somewhere in the craziness of my thoughts I had wished she would have kept us as her family.

That night as I tried to sleep, the only thought that lingered was of Cherlie and my cousin, Peter. Cherlie must have gone looking for Peter to relieve her of her responsibilities of me. But that was understandable. A

person will have you in their house but for so long. Further more if my own mother didn't want to be bothered, who would?
The morning came too soon. I had hoped that it would have lasted just a little longer. But my hope went in vain. Sulei had awoken during the night because she had gone to bed too early that evening. Now she lay asleep while I was awaken by Cherlie. I was awoken not just by her voice but the smell of porridge that she made. From the smell of it I could tell it was cornmeal porridge. Whenever Cherlie made cornmeal porridge she used a lot of cinnamon and vanilla. Her entire house held the aroma of cinnamon and vanilla essence.
"Get up," she said tugging at the blanket that covered me partially. "Remember we're going to see Peter today." Pitching her voice a bit higher she continued, "Furthermore is Saturday. Nobody sleeps this late in my house."
Charlie was a very giving and caring person. I guess I had inconvenienced her son somewhat. Okay, a lot. And I was not the neatest guest you could have. And I did not put things back the way that I found them. And I did not help to clean. She had to ask for my help with the dishes because I was not self-motivated. I was not motivated at all. My mind was in shambles. My whole life was in a state of confusion – one big chaos. I did not know if I was going up or down. So I was of little help to Cherlie, because I was of little help to Sulei and myself.
I needed a break from everything. I needed a break from being a mother. I needed a break from worrying about tomorrow – a break from not knowing where Sulei and I would be tomorrow. It seemed as if what my mother said would actually come to pass, almost prophetically. Amidst my mother's anger she told me that 'she would live to see me living in a shelter', which meant that

eventually that is where I would end up living. And as hard as I had tried to not allow that to ever happen it seemed as though all odds were against me now.

Sulei finally awoke. I fed her some porridge and gave her a bath. Cherlie's porridge was delicious. After getting her dressed Cherlie marveled at her new wardrobe.

"Who bought those for her?" she asked admiring them up close.

"Paul," I lied.

"Paul?" she asked suspiciously while doing the funny thing she does with her eyebrows whenever she knew Patterson was lying.

"Yes," I replied, lying again. I hated lying. But what was I going to say I STOLE THEM. I couldn't. I had to lie.

But from the way she continued to look at me I could tell she did not believe a word I had said. She never did tell me though where she actually thought I had gotten them from, or from whom. But I could tell that she never really believed me.

We left her house in pursuit of Pete thirty minutes later. No one spoke during the ride to his house. Sulei sat quietly on my lap. We sat in the back of Cherlie's car. Cherlie did not allow us to sit in the front, she preferred us in the back so I could hold Sulei firmly, because she did not have a car seat for her.

The car finally pulled up in front of a house. Three men stood in the front of the yard. Two wore dread locked hair and the other had his hair cut low. The elder man with dread locks approached the car.

"Wha'pen?" >>>> (What's up?) He had a deep Jamaican accent.

"Nut'ting," >>>> (Nothing) Charlie answered then looking in the back at Sulei and me.

"A she dat?" >>>>> (Is that her?) He asked as if I was

an orphan or a stray cat. I guess at this point in life I was both.

"Yeh." >>>> (Yes) At that she turned her body around to look at me from a better view, then continued, "Dat's yuhh cousin Pete" >>>> (That's your cousin Pete).

"Hi," I deliberately avoided looking at him. I was embarrassed at what my life had become. Here I was actually begging for a place to stay. That is what my life had become. The sad thing was I had brought an innocent victim into my confused and atrocious life.

"Wheh yuhh name again?" >>>> (What's your name again?) He asked, smiling widely.

"Karlei," I replied as I wrapped my arms closer around Sulei.

"Yuhh a di small one or di big one?" >>>>(Are you the youngest child or the oldest child?) He asked referring to Ilza and me.

"The small one," I responded shuffling my legs to make them more comfortable.

"But yuhh nu did fat, how yuhh get so skinny?" >>>>(Weren't you the fat child? Why are you so thin now?)

"Yeh." >>>>(Yes) I answered softly while slightly blushing. I had surely gotten slim, very slim. I now wore a size six and looked like I was on crack. That's what my suffering did.

"Su wha'pen now, wheh yuhh a sey?" >>>>(So what's up now, what are you saying?) He asked more seriously. Cherlie answered before I could. "She need somewhere to stay. Yuhh nu have a place or room fi har?" >>>>(She is desperately in need of somewhere to live. Do you have a place or room for her?)

"A room? Mek mi see. Yeh, ovah by Monroe Street. Mi have a one bedroom apartment, she can jam deh till she ready" >>>>>(A room? Let me think. Yes, over Monroe Street. I have a one-bedroom apartment, she can stay there until she is ready or until she finds someplace more suitable.)

I was surprise. He just gave me an apartment in his house without any question. This was all too real. Did he really mean it? Just like that? I had known all along that Cherlie wanted me to leave. But I respected her for not putting us out on the streets. Instead, she found a place for us to go.

"When can she move in?" Cherlie asked. They continued with their conversation as if I was not even there.

"Anytime," he replied stepping back from the car.

I was ready to move in today. But I kept silent because no one asked me anything.

"Alright then," starting up the car she lowered her head to make eye contact with him and then continued, "me wid call yuhh later" >>>> (I'll call you later.)

"Okay Karlei, bye baby," he stepped backwards and then waved goodbye to Sulei.

"Okay Pete, bye, thanks a lot." As she slowly drove off she glanced at me in the rear view mirror and then asked, "That's your cousin, you remember him?"

"Yes. I saw him once or twice. I think I saw him once."

"Mmm, he's a very nice man."

"Yeh, it seems that way," I was glad that she asked no more questions because I was too overjoyed to talk. Couple seconds later she broke the silence, "Hungry?"

"Yes."

"Want a beef patty with cocoa bread?" She suggested rather than asked.

"Oh yeah," I was craving for that since the weekend but with no money I had stopped thinking about it.

Her tires rubbed against the side of the pavement as she attempted to park her car. Her car jerked. Muttering something obscene under her breath she got out of the car. Five minutes later she returned with two patties and two bags with cocoa bread. She bought a small red peas (kidney bean) soup for Sulei. I was hungry, but I fed Sulei first. As soon as Sulei had the last spoon of soup I took a bite of the patty. It tasted good. As I bit in the soft yellow crust again the meat rushed into my mouth. She had also bought a cola champagne soda for me. It was a long time since I had one to drink. The thought of having my own apartment reentered my mind. I felt somewhat more at peace than I had felt for a long time. But a deep feeling of fear of not knowing what to expect living alone started building deep within my stomach. But I knew everything would be just fine. I knew Sulei would finally have a room of her own. Peter had said it was a one-bedroom apartment. Although we would both sleep the same room, it would be Sulei's bedroom.

Over the next five days I packed all the clothes that Cherlie gave me, and all of Sulei's clothes. Cherlie helped me move into my new apartment. It consisted of a bedroom, a kitchen and a bathroom. It was not as I had expected. The tiles on the floor in the kitchen were very dirty and most of them were torn. The refrigerator was filled with mini flies. It smelled awful and looked extremely disgusting. I didn't know if I could or would ever clean the refrigerator. It was very polluted. The pipe in the kitchen sink had no water and the sink was dirty. The bathroom tub was worse. The tub took us days to sanitize. But I was destitute. I was desperate. And to me it was a castle. My palace. My home. The wall to the hallway in the bedroom had a big hole. With every touch more sheetrock fell out, making the hole bigger. I decided to use Sulei's poster of Sesame Street to cover it. It worked well.
As I looked around the apartment, I felt pity for Sulei

who just stood innocent to the reality of what our life really was. All she knew was the love I gave her. All she knew was my presence around her. And she felt secure with that regardless of where we lived. But it bothered me. We lived in poverty. I was embarrassed as a mother for not being able to provide for my daughter the way a mother should be able to. When would I be able to give her a home that was really a home? A bed that was her own? A refrigerator that she could open and take out a little box of juice and drink? When? All I could give was love and a roof over her head. To me that was not enough. To her that was more than enough, because she was innocent to the frills society dictates as wealth. All her innocence required was love. And that she received.

There was one closet. It was big enough to be used as a playhouse for Sulei. I somehow wished the house looked more appropriate, but I was thankful anyway. There was a family living in the apartment beneath me. It was a man with his wife and four children. I did not see them very often. Their apartment was in silence except when the children came from school at 3:00 p.m. I would hear them running happily from room to room. Unlike my apartment that held silence most of the time. Each day I realized the difficulty of not having a job with a child to support. I depended on my cousin for food and milk for Sulei. I walked to his home everyday just to get milk and food. Sulei and I had gotten really thin. She was very undernourished. Her bones poked through the sides of her body and her face was slender. My mother had moved from Brooklyn almost three years now. She rented an apartment from her brother, my uncle, in Corona, Queens. Her apartment was very different from the one we had in Brooklyn. Now she had two bedrooms. My brother had his own. Her living room was huge, and so was her dining room. She had bought new furniture and her bathroom looked like a picture from a magazine.

I visited my mother occasionally. She had not changed at all. Her heart was still cold and blistered. She still held onto her frigid character. She still had not asked me to come back home. On one of our visits to her home I somehow had thought she would have asked us to come back. But that was an idle thought.
Compared to my home, her home was a palace. Whenever we visited her, I would watch as Sulei ran around, frolicking on the plush carpet in her living room. Whenever I opened her refrigerator, she had adequate supply of food for her family. I did not even have a refrigerator. I pitied Sulei as I watched her eating a yogurt by mother gave her from the many in her fridge. Whenever we left my mother's home I would steal several single servings of apple juice and applesauce for Sulei without letting her know, because if she knew, she would only allow me to take one, not even two. My mother allowed her husband to take us home. She accompanied him whenever he took us home after our visit. She never came upstairs to see my apartment though. She always stayed in their car.

The Lion and the Mouse

I am trapped
With no way out
I must exchange places
With the little grey mouse
It was the lion who got entangled
And the mouse who dismantled
The rope
I was the lion in Jamaica
With a big roar
Now I'm the mouse who has exchanged places
But a mouse with no hope

The lion
The King of the Jungle
I had it all
Love, family, stability,
Was it all a fasade?

Now I'm the mouse
At the lion's mercy
I've set him free
And yet
No pity, no empathy, no mercy
I'm the mouse in a great big city

I am just a mouse!

CHAPTER 12

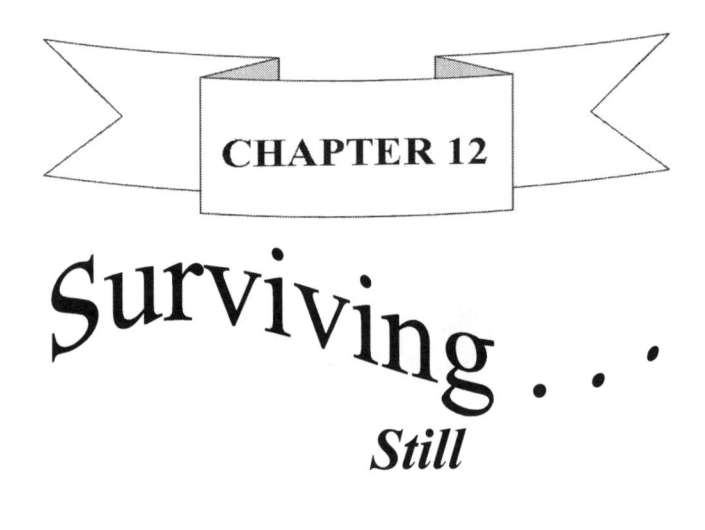

Surviving . . .
Still

Things became worse for us. There were days when Sulei and I had no food to eat or nothing to drink. I would stand at the public phones at the corners of Monroe Street and Nostrand Avenue, pretending that I had just lost my quarter in the phone, the only quarter that I had, and then asked someone, anyone, that happened to walk by for a quarter. Then, when I accumulated enough money I would buy whatever I needed, which was mostly milk for Sulei. Or I would go to the neighborhood supermarket and take whatever I could for Sulei that could easily fit into my pocket. Or I would buy the juice they sold for a 25c and then add water to increase its volume.

I became tired of having to take things that I did not have the money to buy. I wanted to go back to my mother's house, where there was a sense of security. Not just for me but for Sulei. I was on the verge of breaking down, but I knew I had to remain strong for me and for my daughter, but with each day I got weaker, emotionally. In the daytime I would sometimes go to Pete where we would be fed if they cooked. But sometimes they did not cook. Sometimes they bought food at the Jamaican restaurant two blocks away. So sometimes I just remained hungry. The times when the hunger panged at my inside are the times when I desperately yearned to go back home. I thought if I waited a little longer maybe she would ask me back like she did in the past. But it seemed as though I would wait in vain.

I decided that I would not wait any longer for her to ask me to come back home. I would call her instead. Pride tried to hinder me, but my love for Sulei motivated me to call her. Each day as I looked at Sulei, I got more strength to ask my mother to return home. As I walked to the corner of the block where the phone was, I held onto Sulei's hand and prayed for a miracle. I prayed that somewhere in her heart God would place compassion. As I dialed her number my heart fluttered within its cavity from the fear of being told 'no, you can't come back.' I paused before dialing the last number then inhaled deeply.

"Hello," it was her husband.

"Hello, can I speak to my mother please?" I lowered my voice as my heart pounded louder in anticipation of the answer I would get.

As he moved the phone away from his mouth I could hear him whispering, telling her that it was me on the phone. The attitude she came on with I knew I had interrupted 'their precious family time'.

"Hello," she answered bitterly.

"Hello, can Sulei and I come back home?" I asked hoping that her heart had softened during one of our visits to her house.

"No, I don't have any space Karlei. There is no space. You know that. If it was just you, then maybe. But I don't have space for you and a child. Anyway we were just heading through the door. Call back later."

Even though she told me to call back later I knew she didn't mean it. I could hear her telling her husband to 'just hang up the phone.' Her voice held disgust. I could not believe how cold she was. She really had no love for me, or for Sulei. I had called because I was hungry and had nothing to eat. I had wanted to go back home to a warm house and secured meals. But again I was turned away. Maybe now she didn't need a babysitter, so there was no need for me. She had registered my brother in a day care across the street from where she lived. They were opened until 7:00 p.m. The hours were perfect because she reached home at 6:00 p.m. after work. So there was no need for me anymore. As I walked back to where I called home, the tears fell. I

did not care anymore. Even if I did, I could not stop them from falling. As I held onto Sulei's hand, for the first time I felt her sadness. She had never seen me cry. But now she did. And I could see my sadness reflecting on her face as she looked up at my tears, though she never said a word. As we made it inside our 'home', I sat on the bed. The tears rolled uncontrollably down my face. The anguish was difficult to sustain. My hunger increased with every tear that fell.
"Everything will be okay, I promise," I whispered to her. "One day mommy will be able to provide for you better. I'm sorry to bring you into this world like this, but I had planned differently. I love you Sulei. I really love you. I wish I could give you toys to play with. Take you to Toys'R'Us and give you what children your age have. But I can't. All I can give you is love. I can't even provide milk for you sometimes, but I promise that one day I'll make you proud to be my daughter. I'll love you as a mother should love her daughter. I'll give you unconditional love. I'll give you what I've needed all these years from a mother but never found."
I spoke to her as though she understood. But somehow I knew she did. Or maybe I wished she understood.

Never Stop Trying

I swear if it is till the day I die
I will never stop trying
To give you want you need
I will never stop trying
To comfort you indeed
I will never stop trying

I swear on the ground I walk
I'll make sure you are happy
If it's the last breath I take
I'll give you everything you needed
If it is the last thing I do
I'll make it up to you

But I'll never stop trying
To give you the life you should be having
The times you should be playing
On a swing or riding
A bike
Such is life!
But if it's the last breath I take
I swear I'll never stop trying!

CHAPTER 13

SURVIVING...
Barely

The days had begun to get warmer which meant I would have to find summer clothes for Sulei. I could not go back to Marcy's again. I did not want to subject myself to being caught and going to jail. But the truth was I knew I had to find summer clothes for her. I decided that instead of stealing I would just go in, explain my situation to one of the girls at the register and ask her to put a couple pieces of clothing in a bag for Sulei and me. Sounded simple? Yeah right. But I had to try something. Anything.

I could not believe my life had taken this path. Here I was heading to a store to beg for clothes for my daughter. My sister, Ilza would never believe this. As I made my way to Marcy's I became excited for us. Suddenly I changed my mind. Instead I would visit A&V, a store just like Marcy's but it was closer to the train station.

As I entered the store my eyes wandered from rack to rack. The clothes they had out for summer looked expensive. Smiling to the security guard at the entrance I made my way up the stairs to the children's department. There were security guards everywhere. The store was busy with consumers. The cashier that stood at the register attended to the last customer that was on line. I slowly approached her.

"Excuse me Miss," lowering my voice and glancing to see if anyone was approaching.

"Yes," she said firmly with the typical 'sales girl' attitude.

"My daughter and I were kicked out of my mother's house. When we were moving, I rested my bags on the sidewalk and someone moved everything. The bags and all."

She looked at me with disbelief. "Wow. Everything?"

"Everything," I answered emotionally after I remembered that they *had* taken everything, even the pictures I had with Sulei. They even took the ones from her christening. They had taken everything.
"Well, I don't know if they're hiring," she had an accent that I could not detect.
"No, I'm not asking for a job. Can you please put some clothes in a bag for me? Please?" I asked desperately.
"Are you kidding me?" she said barely smiling.
"No."
I could tell she knew I was serious by the way she arched her eyebrows.
"What if you're an undercover store security officer?" Pausing for a brief second she then added, "No. I need my job, I'm sorry." She then allowed her eyes to scan her immediate area to see if there might have been security guards around seeing what her decision would be.
"Okay, thanks anyway. Where are you from?" I was curious to know.
"Panama, and you?" From her response I knew she was becoming a little more relaxed.
"Jamaica. Listen can you please, just one or two pieces please?" I stood there for several minutes before she agreed. Her name tag read, *Annette*.
"Okay, not a lot. You better not be security," the sales girl shot back glancing around the store.
"Are you crazy? Do I *look* like security?" I blurted out.
"Thanks very much, okay?"
I chose four outfits for me that I knew would be able to make other outfits by interchanging them. For Sulei I chose seven outfits and a sneaker. I chose some barrettes for her hair and some socks. I also chose a light jacket for her because the jacket she wore was the one from her snowsuit, which was a little too thick for spring.

As I left the store I was thankful to the sales girl who really helped me out. We spent the rest of the day walking around downtown Brooklyn on Fulton Street. I started getting hungry so I decided to take the train back to Pete's house hoping that they had cooked dinner. I couldn't believe what just happened. Was it God? Would God allow me to steal? Did he understand my situation and allowed me to get away with stealing? I thanked him anyhow.

I Am NOT My Past

Judge if you want
Guess if you want
I am not my past
Just an experience
Snob me if you want
Ignore me if you want
I am not my past
Just resilient

I am different
I have come to learn that fact
I am peculiar
But not society's stats

So judge if you want
Guess if you want
Snob me
Ignore me
But the fact is
I am me
Existing from my experiences

CHAPTER 14

SURVIVING...
The Meeting

As I sat in the living room of my cousin's house, I could hear the voice of several different men approaching. A man that I had never seen before walked passed and headed to the window in the living room. He separated the curtains and peeked outside. As he walked back, he quickly glanced at me. He was in his twenties and not very attractive. He was short with wide shoulders. He paced the floor in the living room as he conversed with Peter. He stayed for about an hour and then left. After he left I asked Peter who he was. His name was Doug. Peter said Doug lived in the Bronx with his sister. I had overheard him telling Peter that his sister's latest beau was taking him to an auction in New Jersey to buy a car. After he left they all discussed how cheap he was and how he was always trying to manipulate people.

I never saw Doug again.

Summer was finally here. I spent the weekends at my aunt's house in Brooklyn. She was my father's sister. I had gotten her number from Peter and called her to let her know I was staying at one of Peter's house. She was much older than I was, but she was very understanding.

The summer after I came to New York to live with my mother, she had taken me on a lot of 'bus rides'. These were trips to different places of attractions coordinated by her friends. She would always invite me and I always went. My mother always agreed to send me. Maybe that was her way of getting rid of me so she could spend quality time with her family.
My aunt cooked and brought everything we needed for the picnic. I enjoyed her company.

When my mother had kicked me out I had wanted to live with her but my mother had threatened to call Immigration to have me deported. So instead I stayed with Ronnie, my mother's sister ex-boyfriend. My aunt still lived in the same apartment building that I had gotten kicked out of when my mother found out that I was pregnant. Now walking back into the apartment building where my mother use to live reminded me of the hurt and pain of the cold November night when I was kicked out.

On one of my visits on the weekend, my aunt took me over to my uncle's apartment. My uncle, Thrums, was my father's brother. Thrums lived in the west wing of the building with his wife, Dee-Dee. Dee-Dee loved Sulei and asked me if she could stay for a weekend as a play date for her daughter Punkie. I agreed as I desperately needed time to think what our next move was.

On the weekends I stayed at my aunt's house while Sulei stayed with Dee-Dee across the hallway. Dee-Dee took admirable care of Sulei. She bought her fine clothing that I could not afford to buy. Whenever I saw Sulei, she always seemed happy. I rarely went to visit her even though she was just across the hall. I could not sustain the anguish of leaving her. So I stayed away. One day after I had visited her I overheard her referring to my uncle and Dee-Dee as 'mommy' and 'daddy', which literally broke my heart. She no longer referred to me as 'mommy' instead she called me Karlei. But I knew even though I wanted to take her so she could call me 'mommy', I resisted the urge. Sulei needed stability, which I could not afford at the time. And furthermore, the time apart gave me time to think what next? But I couldn't help feeling hurt and betrayed although I knew she was only a year old.

My uncle and his wife had started making plans of moving South to Florida. They asked me if they could take Sulei with them when they were leaving, but I could not allow her to go with them. She was all I had. She was my reason for living and the reason I still had my sanity. She was the only reason I had not broken under the circumstances and the pressure that I bore. How could I possibly give up the only true love that I had and known. I had made a pledge that no matter how hard life had gotten I preferred going back home to Jamaica with her rather than to give her away as my mother did Ilza and me. The trend had to be broken somewhere, somehow.

I had stopped calling my mother as often as before. After I had asked her permission to return home and she said no I decided to not call or visit as often as I did before. I had told her where I was on the weekends, and where Sulei stayed, as if she really cared. She thought it was better for Sulei's sake. She said they would take better care of her than I was able to. I thought the nerve of her.

Sulei stayed with them for four months. I got a chance to sign on with Olsten Temporary Service who helped me to find jobs. The wage earned was not much but it was something. I had visited A&V one more time to see the sales girl the week before I started to work. She allowed me to take three suits and a pair of shoes. Those served as my working clothes, the three suits of clothes. I decided to visit my mother on my way from work. I wanted her to see the woman I was becoming. But I could tell she was still the same person, cold and without love. We spoke briefly. During the conversation she told me that she had spoken to my uncle's wife. She told me that she had told her that she should take Sulei with her whenever she moved because I could not properly care for Sulei. I was in total disbelief. Then I became enraged.

How could my mother, my own mother once again fail me? What had I done wrong that she despised me so much?

"Why would you say that to her?" I asked.

But before she could answer, I walked away as fast as I could towards the train station. I had no intentions of giving my daughter away as she did me. I had only needed help. I had only turned to them to help me with Sulei because they were my last resort. I had no intention of letting them keep her. How dare her or anyone else to think otherwise.

"Karlei," she called out as I began to walk away.

"I'm going for my daughter. How could you tell her something like that?"

"I thought..." then she continued, "I thought that would have been best for her," she added.

"What's best for her?" I had wanted to ask. Then I had wanted to say, "You don't have a clue what's best for me or Sulei. No clue. What would have been best was for you as a grandmother to tell me it was okay for me to come back home because of the baby. Just because of Sulei, not me. Not your love for me, but your love for your grandchild. That's what would have been best for us; for you to tell us we could come back home." But I did not have the guts to say it. I did not have the backbone to say what I really thought. I was too scared that I would not get her approval. That was all I ever looked for. I looked for her approval to fulfill the emptiness that dwelled inside me that yearned to be fulfilled, to be loved, to feel wanted, and to belong.

I did not have the courage to tell her that what she had wanted from the beginning was for me to abort Sulei. Or maybe she had wanted me to give her away when she said she only had space for me. Or maybe she had

wanted me to give Sulei away as she had given me away when she said she did not have 'enough' space for two. If I was by myself, she had said, it was okay, but because I had Sulei, she did not have enough space for my baby and me.
I had wanted to say it all, but instead all I said was, "I have to go," and then I walked away. As I walked away I was mad at myself for not being woman enough to say what I really felt. What could she have done that she had not done already? Wished she aborted me? Tell me she will live to see me in a shelter? What? Just what could she have done that she had not done or said already? But even though I knew there was nothing more for her to say or do to hurt me, inside I still hung on to the possibility that one day she would love me.

The walk down 110th Street and Northern Boulevard to 110th Street and Roosevelt Avenue in Corona seemed longer than usual. The train seemed to take forever. Then finally it came. Then the ride seemed to take forever. I had to switch from the 7 train to the D train to Flatbush. Finally it was my turn to get off. As the train came to a halt I impatiently scampered off and made my way to my uncle's house.

I tapped on the door once when it opened slowly. "My mother called you right?" I asked as I entered their house. My uncle was not there. I was delighted, I communicated with his wife better than I did with him. There was something strange about him that I still had not figured out. I then realized that I hadn't even greeted her. I was too upset. I was upset with my mother, myself, and the world.
"Yeh." >>>>(**Yes**) She responded as she sat on the sofa. His wife spoke with a deep Jamaican accent. She was very pretty. She could easily be mistaken for a

descendant of the Native American tribe. Her skin was like a deep chocolate color. She wore the finest clothes and jewelry. She made sure Sulei wore the finest clothes too. She took care of Sulei better than I could. But I wanted my daughter. I didn't trust my mother's motives and now I was not sure if I trusted them with my daughter anymore.

"Did she suggest that you take Sulei with you when you move?" I asked referring to my mother.

"Yeh, a whah?" >>>>> (**Yes, why?**) She seemed confused.

"She told you to take Sulei with you when you move didn't she?" But before she could answer, I continued, "Don't listen to her. As a matter of fact I thank you for all you've done for us but I think I'm going to take her with me now."

My uncle's wife didn't respond. But I knew she thought I was crazy. And I was. I was crazy if I allowed her to take Sulei with her. I knew if I took Sulei I wouldn't be able to work. I knew things would be hard for us again. But that's the risk I would have to take. And that's the choice I made. The money I worked would not be sufficient to pay a baby sitter. No matter how inexpensive they were. But, I wanted my daughter back. I could not live with myself if they left with her and I couldn't find her. She was the only reason I still had my sanity.

She packed all of Sulei's clothes, even the ones she bought. I knew she loved Sulei and had gotten attached to her. But I couldn't risk losing my daughter. I didn't know if I could trust anyone. Not even my mother. They had both apologize for discussing Sulei's future without me knowing. But I still refused to trust their word. And the nerve of my mother. The nerve of her! Not choosing to help us even with a dollar, but have the nerve to suggest that they take her with them when they moved?! Bitterness entrapped my heart in its own world and I began to resent my mother.

After I left, I went over to my aunt's house. I was surprised to know that she was at home. But she was more surprised that I had taken Sulei, because it contradicted everything about my plans that I had told her in confidence. But she understood after I told her what my mother had done. I knew things would eventually get worse for us again but I knew God was on our side. I knew he would not forsake us.

I hadn't been at my apartment for the past two months. Upon returning I could tell someone had entered and ravaged through my things, the little that I had. Nothing was the way I had left them. My uncle and his friends had started to renovate the building also. The building was dusty and dirty from the work they did. Everyday my cousin, Peter, and his three friends worked in the basement.

As I came in the building one day after buying milk for Sulei I ran into Doug coming out of the building. We briefly said hello before I vanished behind the door of the apartment building. But before I could make my way up the stairs I was stopped by Peter who made his way up from the basement.

"What's up, whey yuhh did deh?" >>> (What's up? Where have you been?)

"At your cousin's house," I said referring to my aunt in Brooklyn.

"Oh. Doug. Remembah Doug? Di same manipulatin' one whey visit me di night ovah Madison?" >>> (Remember Doug? The same manipulating one that visited my house on Madison Avenue?)

How could I forget? "Yes."

"He jus' lef'. He was askin' fi yuhh." >>> (He just left. He was asking for you.)

"Oh yea, I just saw him, but he didn't say anything. Why

he asking fah me?" >>> (Why was he asking for me?) "Ah don' know. But anyway, mi hav' a lat of work fi du in a dis basement, su latah. Mi dung stays if yuhh need me." >>> (I really don't know. But anyway, I have a lot of work to do in the basement. So later. I'm down stairs if you need me. Okay?)
As he walked away he muttered that for the past two months Doug came by to visit them occasionally.

Doug's visits became more consistent. During one of his visits we started up a conversation briefly as I exited the building. He was standing on the step outside the front door. He told me he was born in Jamaica. He had left Jamaica at age two. He was twenty-four years old. He had one child, a son. He worked for an insurance firm. His voice was rough and from his vocabulary I could tell he was not very educated. There was something about his character that bewildered me because he never gave eye contact.
After our first conversation I saw him more frequently whenever he came by to visit Peter. Eventually he got up enough courage to invite me out to dinner. I never quite figured the reason I accepted, maybe it was boredom or maybe knowing that I would get a free meal and be able to bring back at least some fries for Sulei. I asked my aunt if Sulei could stay with her for the night. The ride to her house was long, and caused me to regret accepting Doug's invitation to dinner. After I left my aunt's house I went to meet Doug who had agreed to meet me at the Nostrand Avenue station. When I arrived he was already there. He dressed sloppy. His lower body seemed too thin for his broad shoulders. He was not my type. I was embarrassed to even be associated with him. But I knew in his pocket held the money for my dinner.
We took the train to the city. We spoke about nothing

and giggled about foolish things.
Our date lasted approximately three hours. We had Burger King for dinner. That's all I wanted - Burger King. Afterwards he took me home, he insisted to come in but I refused. He was very aggressive, something that I despised in a man especially on a first date. After he left I realized what my life had really become. A date with a man I despised just to secure a meal.
I never called him back again. He couldn't call either, because my phone got disconnected because I was unable to pay the bill. Again.
I decided to wait in the morning to travel to my aunt's house for Sulei. It was too late, and I hated traveling the train at nights. There were too many homeless men and women and crack heads on the streets. I was homeless too. But the difference was I wasn't on crack and I looked and smelled clean.

CHAPTER 15

SURVIVING...
The Landslide

Things did get worst. We were back to where we had started. There were days when I had nothing to eat. This time, however, I made sure Sulei was fed properly. She ate mostly chicken liver for dinner, since that was one of the cheapest choices in the supermarket. Keyfood Supermarket sold it for a dollar. She had gained some weight while living with my uncle and his wife, and I refused to let her become thin again.

After Peter and his workers left each day and Sulei went to bed, I would run to the basement to see what food I could find. For lunch, they bought food from the Jamaican restaurant three blocks away from the apartment. After they left I would go to the basement to eat whatever was left because most times they did not eat it all. Whatever was left in their containers would then become my dinner. The food was always good. They mostly ate oxtails or curry goat. Their leftover would always have meat but seldom had rice. I would always have to combine two or three of their lunches to have adequate rice for the meat. I would sometimes wonder if they figured out that I ate their food after they left at nights or they thought there were mice in the building. Normally I took the food upstairs to my apartment. But this particular night after getting the food that they had left in the basement, I was too hungry to take it upstairs so I stood in the basement and gorged it down. Food never tasted better. The curry goat was unusually spicy though, which made me extremely thirsty. As I searched for any soda that might have been left I spotted a large soda bottle sitting on the makeshift desk against the wall. I was ecstatic. Picking up the bottle, I was delighted that only half was gone. I quickly held it to my mouth and took a big gulp. I was horrified! It was not soda, but rather a cleaning agent. It smelled like Pine Sol!

The reality of what my life was became clear to me then. There was no worse that things could possibly get. This was the worst. And I had to get out of it. I had lost a tremendous amount of weight. I looked as though I had started to abuse drugs, maybe crack. I looked pitiful. I had no butt. I was just flat. No breast, no butt. I had lost it all. I slowly walked back up the stairs. I was numb. I wanted to cry, but no tears came. I was ashamed and embarrassed at what I had become. I was at the lowest that I thought possible. I was homeless and without food.

Sulei was awake when I got back upstairs. It must have been about eight o'clock. The nights didn't get dark too quick anymore now that summer was finally here. I decided to take a walk to my cousin's house. I knew Sulei would soon be hungry. Putting on her clothes, we sang 'It's A Small World Afterall', even though I did not know all the words.

As we walked slowly, I wished that I had a stroller for her. That would have made things a lot easier. But I didn't and had to make the most of what I had – my feet and arms. I carried her on my hips the entire journey. My arms ached but I kept going anyway. He lived twelve blocks from my home, and they were long blocks.

My cousin was standing at the door when we arrived. He always stood at the door to get 'fresh air'.

"Wha'pen, how yuhh outside su late wid di baby?" >>>>(What's up, why are you out this late with the baby?) He asked concerned.

Shrugging my shoulders I said I did not know. But in fact I really did know. I knew she would soon become hungry and I had no food to give her. So I came to his house to get something for her to eat.

"Come in nu," >>>> (Come on in) he said pointing to the living room, and then disappeared behind the wall.

The sound of his footsteps escaped in the distant as he made his way upstairs. I had only been upstairs once or twice when he took me to introduce me to two men whom he said knew my father. One of the men was referred to as Shut. In Jamaica, shut means shirt. I never asked why they referred to him as such but can only imagine the story behind his name. Jamaicans have vivid stories for the nicknames people assumed.

Peter returned about twenty minutes later. Then he finally asked if we wanted some dinner. Trying not to sound desperate, I asked what they had cooked, as though it mattered. They'd cooked Sulei's favorite meal, oxtail. I fed her and then she fell asleep. I ate whatever was left. I thought about the walk back to our home and how wearisome it would be, so I decided to spend the night. Furthermore I knew if I spent the night I was sure to have breakfast in the morning. There was nothing for breakfast at my home.

We slept peacefully on the sofa.

The morning sun's rays gleamed brightly through the blinds at the window forming a pattern on the wall above the sofa. It lit up Peter's entire living room. I had missed seeing the gleam of the sun in the mornings because Sulei's bedroom had no windows. There were no sun's rays to brighten her room. I kept the television on throughout the night as a light. I used the lamp that I had found there when I moved but it had no shade and the heat of the bulb had burned one side of the television. The television still worked though, so I used it as light. Whenever we watched the television I had to use a fork as an antenna so the pictures would show more clearly and for more channels to be shown.

We spent the entire day at Peter's house. Sulei and I slept most of the day. We woke just in time to eat the lunch Peter prepared. She must have stayed awake for two hours and then went back to sleep. She was always very quiet. She mostly sat and observed. I was happy for that especially when I had a lot on my mind to think about. As I sat on the sofa I searched my pocket. I had seven dollars. Peter had given me $20.00 last Saturday. All I had remaining was $7.00. I did not know when I would get any more money, so I budgeted myself. But now I needed to buy more milk and juice before going home, because we had none.

The clock above the sofa made me know it was 9 p.m. The day had drifted away so quickly amidst the jokes shared and issues discussed amongst Peter and his friends. But I knew it was time for me to go home. I hated going back to our apartment that was filled with dust from the construction in the basement. But that was our home. The walk home was quiet. I was a small dot in the world. No one knew me. No one knew my name as I walked on my block. I was just a 'she' or a 'her'. As I walked home I observed the many groups of teenagers either in the park or at the corner of a block. They argued, joked, or conversed. I had no one. I was just surviving from day to day. I just existed.

There was no lock on the door so I just pushed it open. Sulei complained of thirst. I had bought her powdered milk because we did not have a refrigerator. Picking up the can I could see that the milk was finished. I had forgotten to buy the milk and juice.

Even though it was late I had to go back outside. I quickly put on Sulei's clothes and jacket and hoped that a store was still open. It was 10:00 p.m. The supermarket at the corner was already closed. But the Chinese restaurant was still open. I doubted that they sold milk. But I still intended to ask them. Sighing, I pushed the glass door opened with my elbow while Sulei lay her head on my shoulder.

"Do you have, I mean, do you sell milk?" I asked the short lady that stood behind the glass before I had even reached the counter.
She did not seem to understand at first, but then she said "no".
I assumed she was Chinese. I could have been wrong because I still could not differentiate between Chinese or Korean. I knew there was a difference, but I could not tell the difference.
Where would I get milk for Sulei at this time of the night? Most of the stores were already closed. The guy at the far right continued to stare. Then I realized it was Doug. He had been admiring me all along.
"What's up?" He seemed so ill mannered. He was everything I did not like and nothing I liked. His English seemed limited and his stare seemed imprudent. His body language was sluggish and his attitude phlegmatic.
"Well?" he continued, he sounded more uncultured than when we had spoken before.
"Oh, nothing," I answered holding my head down, afraid of being associated with him. But then I continued, "I was here to get some milk but apparently they do not sell it," then I walked away.
"This time of night?" he asked as if suggesting that I was lying.
"Yes. Why?"
I did not wait long enough for him to respond before walking away. I had not noticed that he had followed me across the street and kept following me to my house. Turning around to face him I asked him what he wanted.
"Nothing. Who you live with?" he asked bluntly.
"Excuse me?" I asked annoyed.
I could tell he finally got the message. He slowly walked away after looking at me with disbelief because of how I answered him. He seemed very inquisitive. He was

very rude, ill mannered, and I didn't want to be bothered.

CHAPTER 16

SURVIVING...
Looking Up

Two weeks later Doug called. He had gotten my new number from Peter. At first I was upset that he called my house but he asked me to 'hear him out'. He was interested in taking me out on a date again. He apologized for his rude behavior at our last encounter. We spoke for about two hours about nothing. He called me every night after he came home from work.

Four months and a million calls later I took Doug up on his offer to go on a date again. Sulei stayed with my aunt again while Doug and I went to the movies. Then we went to a small deli on the corner of 42nd Street in Manhattan. Our date ended with us returning to his house. I called my aunt to let her know that I would not be coming home. I spent the night over Doug's house. Doug's sister was vacationing in Jamaica. Her picture hung above the fireplace in their living room. She was petite. She was the female version of Doug. His son's picture was on the farther left hand side of the mantle and his mother's picture on the right.
His son was a miniature version of him. He looked everything like Doug. His mother was lighter in complexion and was much shorter. She was of medium built. She now lived in Jamaica. Doug said she retired two years ago.
His room showed signs of bachelorhood all over it. There was nothing female about it. No proper curtains at the window, just a sheet that he used to keep the light out. And his clothes were loosely thrown over the back of his headboard. He kept his furniture clean though. And everything appeared to be where they ought to be. There was an empty bedroom next to his that his sister occupied before his mother moved back to Jamaica. Now she occupied her mother's apartment on the first

floor.

Ideas formulated in my head as I envisioned Sulei and myself living there. The room next to Doug's was big enough for her, and a bed was already in it. I had to somehow get Doug to see that. I had to make him see that his home should be our home too. I did not love him nor did I intend to love him. I just wanted a home for Sulei and a secured lifestyle. Doug was the perfect candidate.

The night seemed to take forever as I lay restlessly on Doug's bed. I worried about Sulei throughout the entire night. I worried about leaving the tranquil surrounding of his home in Queens to go back to the reality of my life in Brooklyn. Queens was quieter. I worried about him saying no to us moving into his home. I worried about everything throughout the entire night.

The morning found me in Doug's bed, the last place I wanted to be. We spoke throughout the night and then he must have fallen asleep. He decided not to go to work. He made breakfast for me. Although he was not my type, I must admit, I was impressed that he hadn't tried having his way with me. I knew if he had tried my plans for Sulei would have come to a halt.

I spent the entire day in his bed watching television. This was the first time since I left Cherlie's house that I felt some sort of comfort. I did not have to worry what to eat or drink. I knew somehow I would make his home my home.

But the comfort came to an end at 4:30 p.m. I knew I had to go for Sulei. I needed her in my life. I had slept in my clothes and Doug was okay with that. I searched his refrigerator for snacks for Sulei before leaving.

Saying goodbye to Doug as I boarded the 'C' train was distressing, because I feared that he would not see things the way I did. I was determined to make his home, our

home. I was determined to make Doug see that we could be a family together. I wanted Sulei to have the best. His house was not a palace, but compared to the apartment I had at my Peter's house, it was a mansion. Throughout the ride home all I could think of was the comfort of Doug's house. I felt a new day of hope beginning for Sulei. I knew that I would somehow move in with Doug and give Sulei the life I promised her. My steps quickened as I walked towards my building. Brooklyn did not seem so enticing anymore. I had to move to Queens somehow. And I knew I would.
As I opened the door, the phone rang. I knew it was my aunt.
"Hello," I grabbed it before having the chance to close the door.
"Hello," the person on the other end answered. It was Doug.
"Just checking to see if you went straight home. Was the train okay?" he asked somewhat concerned.
"Yes, it was all right," I replied. It felt good to have someone who cared or even if it seemed that way.
"Okay then, later." He had no manners what so ever. He just hung up the phone. He always did that. After saying goodbye he just slammed the phone down on the receiver.
Whenever Doug asked me out, I would always refuse. I did not want to leave Sulei again. Wherever I was going, if I would ever go, she would have to come with me, or I would not be going at all. And if Doug could not include her in our plans, then there would be no plan at all. He would just have to understand that I was a package. I did not come alone. I came with a bonus, and that was my daughter. One unit. Complete.

CHAPTER 17

SURVIVING...
A New Morn

Doug persisted, I kept refusing. Eventually, I got up the courage to tell Doug I couldn't leave Sulei. Okay, I lied. I told him my aunt wouldn't baby-sit anymore. But it worked though.

Eventually Doug understood. We all went out together as a unit. A family. Complete.

And eventually we moved in with Doug! Okay, we sneaked up on Doug. Sulei and I went out as often as we could with Doug. Until one day, we never bothered leaving his home to go back to ours. And one day after he left for work, we went to get our stuff in Brooklyn. And since that day we lived at Doug's house.

Sulei spent her 2nd birthday at Doug's house. She made friends with the neighbors' children. She was finally happy. She was finally secured.

Doug supported us financially. He was also a good cook. But he also was very obsessed and overprotective of me. He was very controlling. Before Sulei and I went anywhere we had to ask his permission.

At first I was overwhelmed by his concern. I was flattered to see his curiosity about where we were every minute of the day. Because since I left my mom's home I never really had anyone who cared where I went. I was free as a bird.

At first I thought it was love, but then it became ridiculous. At first I thought it was cute and all, but then I got sick and tired of it.

I had started calling my mother again after Doug left for work. I did not know how to tell her about Doug. I didn't know how to tell her that I had moved in with a man. As if she would even care. But it bothered me to know that I would have to tell my 'mother' I lived with a man. I thought I would tell her about it during one of our conversations one day while visiting her. But instead, she found out about me moving in with Doug during a conversation I had with my aunt, her sister Martha that had just come from Jamaica.

We were always very close, Martha and I. Martha was my mother's sister. They had the same mother, but different fathers. Martha gave me advice on the good things, bad things, and other things of life. She was one of those aunts. One that was a little too down to earth for a mother's sake. She was a kind of aunt that told you the facts of life uncensored. She was a kind of aunt that you could confide in about anything and everything.

She had called my mother to inquire about me. My mother had given her my address and she had visited me in Brooklyn. I was no longer living there. So she had called back to leave a number and I answered the phone. I could not believe she was finally here in America. I was elated. As we conversed on the phone at my mother's house, it just so happened that in excitement, I told her that I had met Doug and would be moving in with him soon. I had spoken aloud, and my mother over heard. I was somewhat embarrassed for her to know I lived with a man.

My aunt and I spoke for about one hour before promising to make a date to see each other the following weekend. We exchanged numbers.

Martha and I spoke several times afterwards. But then our phone stopped working for two days. Doug tried fixing it, but failed. Ultimately, he gave up and called the phone company. The next appointment was two days away. He decided to use his sister's phone until ours was repaired.

He called every day to make sure I was home. If I went to the store, he needed an explanation. If he called and I was unable to answer the phone because of Mother Nature he would accuse me of lying that I was not home. Things started to get unbearable with him. I kept on

denying the fact that he had a problem. I kept fooling myself that this was love; I kept telling myself that I was just not use to having true love like this. I began feeling afraid of being alone again. I was afraid of being homeless again. Afraid of not having anywhere for Sulei to call 'home'. So I decided to 'understand' his ways to keep a roof over our heads.
The phone rang about three times as I hastily picked it up, "hello," I answered between breaths.
"Hello," it was a woman. "Who's this," she asked curiously.
"Karlei."
"Who?" She asked curiously.
"Karlei," I repeated.
"I think I must have the wro….."
Before she could finish I interrupted, "who do you want?"
"Is there a Doug living there?" She asked doubtfully.
"Yes, but he is not here now. Care to leave a message?" I only asked to be inquisitive. I wanted to know who was calling. I was not insecure or jealous, the woman in me was just inquisitive.
"Mary," she said matter-of-factly.
It was his son's mother. I had hoped that she would call one day when he was not there. I had so many unanswered questions that I needed to be answered, but was afraid to ask because of Doug's new temperament. His temper soared easily and his patience was shortened.
"Oh, hi. Doug told me about you. All good," I added quickly, giggling. Hoping to remain on her good side.
"Oh," from her reply I knew she knew nothing of me or who I was to Doug. If I knew Doug well and if my knowledge of his character was factual then he said nothing to no one. I was his new 'secret' that everyone would eventually find out about.
"You're Junior's mother, right?" I asked trying to sound

somewhat friendlier.
"Yes. And you? Who are you to Doug?"
"Me? Well I guess you could say his girlfriend," That was pitiful. I did not even know how to classify our relationship. And here I was living in his house. I guess I felt that way because I knew I had thrown us on him. He had not asked us to live there with him. I had imposed on his bachelor-hood. And the truth was I did not want a relationship, I had only wanted a home for Sulei.
"Oh," she replied coldly.
I knew it was time to say goodbye. Our conversation was going nowhere. She did not care much for a conversation with me and I definitely would not attempt to do otherwise.
Intentionally I forgot to tell Doug that Mary called. But he knew any way because she called later that night and asked him who I was. I never knew what his reply was. He never told me and I never forced the issue. Mary never called back. I waited each day for her to call but she never did. Each time the phone rang I would eagerly reach for it hoping it was her calling, but each time I would be disappointed.

CHAPTER 18

SURVIVING...

The Untold Truth

Finally she did. Mary called again. Two weeks later. We spoke for one and a half hour. She had lived with Doug for two years in the same house that I now lived. She moved out one day while Doug was at work. She said Doug abused her physically. She said he was possessive and controlling. The words struck a chord. Not the physical abuse part, but her words of his possessiveness and controlling behavior certainly did hit a chord. If the others were true because I knew them to be facts, was the physical abuse part true also?
I suddenly questioned myself what had I gotten into? Would he physically abuse me too? Our conversation ended with her promising to call me back with more news of who Doug really is.
When Doug returned from work, my attitude was obviously different. He kept commenting on the visible difference. It bothered me throughout the night even though I tried to put it in the back of my mind. If it was true, why did I keep attracting these types of men? First it was Paul who raped me, now Doug?

Eventually I got over the fear and doubts of what Mary had said. Don't we always do that? Isn't it a shame? Actually it's pathetic. Some women, such as myself, have such low self-esteem that it takes a whole lot to validate our beauty, intelligence, wisdom, and can-do-better-by-myself attitude. I was guilty of that. My granddaddy always told me he loved me and I always heard how 'nice' I was. But nothing was ever validated in stone to enhance my self-esteem. So here I was like millions of other women, craving for poisonous love. Six months later, Doug proposed to me. And guess what? I accepted. Surprised? Is your mouth open yet? Are you saying, 'Dumb' 'Stupid'? Was I dumb and stupid!

I accepted even though I thought it too soon. Like Doug, I had my own agenda. But maybe now I would be able to get my green card. And further more he showed no signs of being abusive, except when I stayed out at the supermarket longer than I should. Or if I decided to visit one of my friends or a relative he had not met, then he went berserk. He would say curse words that were used in Jamaica, and frequently used the f--- word. Unless he was provoked, he showed no sign of impassioned anger. But other than that he was fine.

I must admit though, that sometimes I felt as though I walked on broken glass whenever he came home. A fear overshadowed me continuously, the fear of him being abusive and the fear of him losing control. Of him not having control of himself, and then I would often wondered if Mary had spoken the truth because there were times when one wrong word would cause an eruption of his anger.

CHAPTER 19
THE BEGINNING
Of An End

The day finally came for Doug and I to get married. We had gone two days earlier to City Hall for our marriage license. I was hesitant but Doug consoled me. Doug bought me a green skirt suit two weeks before from a little store on our block. No man had ever bought me anything, so I was overjoyed. I cherished the suit. It was simple but different than anything I had owned. It had satin and lace all over the top of the shirt and on the bottom of the skirt. He decided to wear his blue cotton trousers and white shirt. I was very nervous.
We took the train to the city.
There were brides wearing wedding gowns. Photographers were actually hired. There were brides who were in fact excited because it was their 'big day'. But I was doubtful about getting married. My motivation was the fact that I would convince Doug to sponsor me as his wife, finally getting a green card so I could work and take better care of Sulei.
As I stood against the wall observing the ecstatic brides, I couldn't help feeling sorry for myself. I really could learn how to love Doug but he had no plans for a future. He just lived his life from one day to the next. And his idea of a future included going back home to Jamaica to live within the next five or six years to tend to his cows. He had bought twenty cows with his tax return two years ago. And that was his future plans – to go back to Jamaica to tend to his cows. That was his joy and happiness and the only thing he seemed committed to. We had two different ideas of what happiness should be and what commitment was.
The couple ahead of us was just called in and returned back within fifteen minutes. It was that quick. And I couldn't help but wonder what kind of vows was said in just fifteen minutes. It was no wonder then that the rate

of divorce had escalated so rapidly over the past year. No one took the vows seriously. How could they? Fifteen minutes? That was not even enough to think about the 'for better or worst' part of the vow.
I never quite understood that part of the vow. The 'for better' part, yes I could understand. That was being optimistic. But the 'for worst' part, I just could not understand. Or maybe I did not want to understand that part. Why enter a relationship with that concept. My mother often said, one thing in life she needs no help in doing, and that was doing 'bad' in life. She could do a great job of doing bad all by herself. She needed no help. Would I be lying then if I said 'I do'? It did not matter because I knew I was lying to say I do to 'do you take this man to be your lawful wedded husband? To love....' and we all know the rest, don't we? The truth was I needed a green card.
Just then our names were called. Sulei had been sleeping all this time. My arms ached from her weight, and Doug never once offered to assist. Entering the office, we were escorted into a smaller room that had a bench to the right of the room. I gently placed Sulei down on the bench then stepped towards the man that stood to the left of the room.
"Are you Doug Martin?" He asked turning towards Doug.
"Yes," Doug replied smiling.
Turning towards my direction he asked the same question, "and you, you're Karlei?"
"Yes I am," I answered while noticing his attire.
He was short with a thick mustache that covered most of the top of his lip and his voice was low toned. He wore a black suit with white shirt and a collar that signified he was a clergyman.
"Okay then, let's get started." With that he proceeded with the ceremony, but he had to stop because we had

not come prepared. We had no witness. He sent us to look for a witness. We were forced to ask someone we didn't even know to be our witness. She gladly accepted. She was from Columbia. Listening carefully to the vows that the clergyman read, though he raced through it, I writhed as he read the 'for better or worst'. But answered 'I do' when it was my turn just to get it over with.

The truth is, I had changed my mind the minute I entered the building, but Doug assured me that everything would be fine. And I had hated the fact that we used a total stranger as our witness. But I went along with it. But now here we were standing together being told that we were husband and wife, and that I should kiss him. ***That*** I was not going to do. At no cost. If that was the proof to get a marriage certificate, guess what? We weren't going to get any. I did not kiss Doug because I just could not.

As we left our 'wedding', we headed for our 'honeymoon', a pizza shop a block away. We each got one slice and a soda. Sulei slept throughout the entire ceremony, but was now awake. She enjoyed our reception.

I could complain that my life was empty but I kept reminding myself where we were coming from, and tried not to be ungrateful to the Lord. I remembered praying many nights for someone to love me and to love Sulei. I guess my prayer was not detailed enough about the specifics of the love I searched for.

Riding the train home I realized that indeed there was a problem within me, because I never felt free to love or to trust anyone. I could never genuinely love anyone but my daughter. And I had the fear constantly of someone betraying my love and trust. I could never fully give my all to anyone. As I looked across at Doug, I knew he too had issues of emptiness that stemmed from his childhood. He had issues of emptiness that originated from his mother preferring his sister to him, as he often spoke of.

I had come to realize over the past months that Doug had deep topics in his life that were unresolved. He was seeking for somewhere to belong and someone to belong to. Someone that would not fail him as his mother had allegedly done by giving more love to his sister than to him. A feeling of compassion overcame me suddenly. And for the first time I saw him differently.

I wanted to tell him everything would be okay and that I loved him. I wanted to explain to him the reason for me not kissing him today. Not because I did not love him but because I just couldn't. Maybe I was just too shy or I wasn't prepared for it. But it had nothing to do with love. But that would all be a lie and I would only say it to console him.

He kept staring through the window of the train or so it seemed until I saw the truth. He was watching me all along through the window that created a mirror from the darkness of the tunnel that we went through. He had wanting in his eyes. Wanting to be needed and cared for. But I couldn't tell him I love him. I couldn't tell him any of the things I wanted to tell him because they were lies. All lies. I did not love him then and I know I would never love him. And I knew I would not have even tried to love him. I knew the truth was all I wanted was my green card. All I cared about was Sulei's happiness.

Walking off the train together with Sulei in my arms he never once suggested for him to carry her instead. He just kept walking two feet ahead of me all the time. I despised the coldness of his character and heart. There was no love felt from him. But maybe he was cold because of his experiences in life. Or maybe I was cold and without heart. Maybe he knew that I didn't love him. I really didn't care about love. All I wanted was for him to be warm and kind enough to help me with Sulei. So I had not even cared enough to hear him tell me he loved me. Because the truth was I did not even know what to look for in a man or what were the characteristics to seek for.

Being married to Doug was more fatiguing than I had anticipated. He gave me $30.00 every two weeks to shop for whatever I needed and to buy groceries for the house. But it was more than I had when I lived in Brooklyn. Doug expected me to have dinner prepared and waiting when he came home from work. He expected to have a full course meal. I felt pressured and stressed to prepare meals everyday from $30.00 per week for two weeks.

After Doug left for work each day, I was left alone in the house. It wasn't a mansion, but it was big enough to feel alone. His sister was rarely home. And whenever she was home, we seldom spoke. She was left in charge of the house after their mother retired in Jamaica.

She conferred with Doug that she had decided to rent the second floor apartment, which was empty. The previous tenant had moved. She had saved and bought a house. She told Doug that one of their mother's friends referred a suitable tenant for the apartment. Doug said it was a Jamaican couple and a baby. They needed the apartment as soon as possible. His sister allowed them to view the apartment. Unfortunately I had gone to the supermarket when they had come so I had not seen them. The man's name was Gary, his wife's name was Tiffany.

CHAPTER 20

BROAD HATS & LONG SKIRTS

*It's All In The Church &
So is Everything Else*

The day finally arrived for the new tenants to move in. They had only been married for two years. They had lived apart since getting married because he lived in America, and she lived in Jamaica. But now she was finally here with him. She had come to live with him in America about two weeks ago. I was curious to see what she looked like. Upon hearing her in their bathroom discussing the color scheme, I decided to walk downstairs. As I passed them I greeted them. I was astonished. She looked so young. She could not have been any older than eighteen. He on the other hand looked somewhere in his thirties. He seemed much older than she was. She held a little baby in her arms on her side.
As I passed, she smiled. Her smile was childish too. As we greeted each other, I introduced myself. Her name was Tiffany and her husband's, Gary.

They were Christians. Every Sunday they went to church. Tiffany and I became very close friends. I shared all my secrets with her. And she shared some of her secrets with me. I told her that I did not love Doug and she told me she did not love her husband either. I was in shock to hear of a Christian not loving her husband. But I guess she was human after all. Her daughter Tammy became friends with Sulei. Tiffany became more like a sister to me than a friend. She constantly invited me to church but I never went. Occasionally she took Sulei with her to church. Sulei loved going to church and kept asking me to go, but I refused.

While in Jamaica I attended a Pentecostal church on Wildman Street with our neighbors, The Carters. On

Saturdays they would wash Ilza's and my hair and twist it, preparing us for church. We always participated in the Christmas programs at their church. We both went until we were old enough to decide which church we wanted to go, if any at all. I continued, but Ilza stopped attending. That's when I decided to get baptized at 13 years old. But then I left and came to America. I never found a church that could compare to the church in Jamaica until Tiffany came to live at Doug's house and I finally went with her one day. And though I went, I was not ready to 'dedicate' myself to the Lord as yet.

Tiffany and Gary lived at the apartment for four years. Everything went well until one of the pipes in Tiffany's kitchen sink had a leak. Doug's sister hired a man to fix the leaky faucet that Tiffany had complained about for months. Finally it was scheduled for a man to fix the leaky faucet. The morning the man came, Doug's sister took him to Tiffany's apartment. Tiffany must have been asleep because she did not hear Jan knocking her door several times.
Tiffany must have awoken during the knocking but Jan had already opened the door and entered with the man following behind her. Tiffany was still in her nightgown that was made of a sheer material. Embarrassed and alarmed, Tiffany screamed as loud as she could. She was extremely upset that Jan had brought the man into her apartment and she was not properly dressed. Jan and the man left without fixing the faucet, but that's where the division started between Tiffany and me.
Later that night, Tiffany told Gary what had happened. She had confided in me that she would have told him. I did not dissuade her. Gary was intensely perturbed. I had never before heard him scream or even talked so loud, but now his voice echoed throughout the entire house.

"Listen, excuse me, Jan," he screamed storming out of his apartment heading for Jan's apartment.
"Excuse me," he continued as he knocked vigorously on the door.
But Doug answered instead, "What is it?" he asked ill-mannered as usual.
"My wife was in the house, and your sister bring man in the house on her, and she was in her nightgown, she didn't even knock," Gary's voice shook as he spoke as he rambled on.
The argument escalated. Everyone was shouting except Tiffany and me. Doug had known about the incident. Jan had told him about it soon after he came home from work. He had commented that he would wait for Gary to approach him to 'blast his soul straight to hell'.
After the confrontation, nothing was the same anymore. Tiffany and I seldom spoke.

Two months later they decided to move. After Tiffany moved, I never heard of her again. The apartment stayed vacant for six months. My days were not excited anymore. I realized then how close I had gotten to Tiffany.

CHAPTER 21

A NEW CHAPTER

Doug had already left for work and I finally went back to sleep, but was disturbed when the phone rang. As I rolled over to answer the phone I wondered who would be calling this early in the morning. Struggling to put the phone at my ear before the caller hung up I babbled into the earpiece instead.

"Hello," I managed to mutter as I placed the phone correctly to my mouth.

"Hello," it was my mother. She sounded excited.

"Hello," I repeated.

"Yeah, I just get a call from Jamaica. Chez got a visa to visit Disney World with her school. She's going to Florida next week."

Chez was the second youngest girl child for my mother. When my mother had found out that I was pregnant she had told me that she wished Chez was here instead, and not me. Her words had cut deep and had scarred every tissue that covered my bones. The depth of my mother's love then had been apparent, and showed that it was shallow with love for me. It was evident that there had been no depth to her love at all. Facing the truth was the hardest. Hearing her saying the words was difficult, but actually knowing that her words were filled with truth hurt even more. And now to hear the excitement that filled her voice brought pain again. I knew my mother would never love me the way I really wished for her to love me. I knew she would never have the unconditional love for me that I felt for Sulei. But somewhere deep inside I had carried the hope, but now it seemed useless.

Chez came two weeks later. She was tall and thin. She had the body structure of a model. She was beautiful. Much more than I was. And sometimes looking at her I wished I could have what she had. Her looks, her body

structure, but most of all the love she received from my mother. Chez and I had not seen each other for six years. Now we tried to reminisce about our childhood. I told her about Doug, she told me about her crush on a boy named Charles back in Jamaica. But it was obvious that the sisterly love was missing. After all it had been six years, and we never kept in touch. I was too busy surviving. She was too busy wishing to be here with a mother she didn't know had grown cold like the bitter cold day in December amidst a winter storm.
I was glad that Chez came because I was empty since Tiffany had moved. Chez and I spoke constantly on the phone. She visited me often at Doug's house. She did not care much for Doug but Chez was happy for me if I was happy with Doug. I never did clarify my feelings for Doug that all I wanted was a life for Sulei and Doug held the key to the possibility - a green card. Our house seemed empty after Tiffany moved. My only source of friendship was Chez.

Eventually Doug's sister rented the apartment to someone else. Her name was Beauty, and she was middle aged. She lived alone. She had three children that she had left in Jamaica with their grandmother in the hope of coming to America to find gold.
She had no green card either. She worked as a waitress at a Jamaican restaurant on Francis Lewis Blvd. She worked at nights and slept throughout the day. Inside her apartment was filled mostly with silence during the day. Periodically we would speak about the weather and Sulei, whom she admired, whenever we saw each other in the hallway. Doug seldom spoke to her, which she found unusual and commented about it very often. Her Jamaican accent was very evident.
"How come 'im suh kumoojin?" >>>> (Why doesn't he speak to anyone?) She questioned, rolling her eyes.

"I don't know," I replied laughing.
"'Im tan too bad mon," >>>> (He has a bad attitude) she continued.
"That's Doug for you, Beauty."
"Jesus mon, 'im can at least sey hi when 'im pass people pan di step," >>>> (He can at least say hi whenever he passes someone on the stairs), she said filled with detestation.

Beauty was always like that since she came to live in the house. She never held back anything she had to say. She just said whatever was on her mind. Sometimes I think she didn't think before she spoke. And sometimes I wish I were like her in that way. But deep inside I wished she would stop wanting Doug to say hi. I felt as though she admired him or was attracted to him. But she didn't stop asking and eventually it didn't bother me as much.
Speaking to Beauty was very fulfilling. I had expressed my desire to work one day while we converse. She had promised to ask her boss about a position for me, which seemed to take forever. I questioned her about the progress she was making getting me a job. Eventually she saw the seriousness of my desire to work and made an extra effort.
But many months would pass before she actually made it possible for me to be interviewed. I told Doug nothing about it until two days before the interview. He resented my relationship with Beauty and had commented on the different male friends of hers that visited her regularly. Beauty had many male friends or so she classified them. But I didn't care. I only cared about getting a job and providing proper care for Sulei. I also cared about not being able to get the job because I didn't have a green card. I worried constantly that I would be asked for proof of residency. But nothing tried, nothing

accomplished.

The day for the interview finally arrived.
Anxiety overshadowed me as I entered the restaurant. It was small and cozy. There were eight or nine tables in the dining area. Each table had four chairs except the round table in the center, which had five. There were plants all over the dining room and paintings hung on the walls. The paintings had 'for sale' signs posted on them. The man at the register fitted the description Beauty had given me of the owner's nephew, Thomas.
He was tall and very muscular. His hair was cut very low. As I approach him closer, I got a better view of his eyes. They were more beautiful than they had appeared from afar. His lips looked tantalizing. They looked soft and moisturized. He seemed well taken care of.
"Yes, may I help you," he said abruptly.
"Yes, I spoke to someone named Thomas on the phone on Thursday three days ago and he told me to come in for an interview," stumbling nervously over my words while trying to remain calm.
"Yes, I'm Thomas, just have a seat and I'll be right with you," he had a Jamaican accent but he spoke more English than Jamaican patois.
As I sat and waited, the other waitresses stared curiously at me as they went to and from the dining room serving customers. The waiting was the hardest part. I did not know where to put my hands or how to sit. Finally he came over after being relieved by a young woman who came from the basement.
While sitting I admired the pictures on the wall that made a huge collage. I recognized Shabba, the Jamaican singer. Next to him was Bizmarkie, LL Cool J, Salt from Salt-n-Peppa, and other faces that I didn't know, but knew they were famous for something or their picture would not be on the wall.

"Wha' tek yuhh su long mon?," >>>> (What took you so long?) he asked, but she did not reply. She just looked at him scornfully and kept walking.

"Sorry about that, what was yuhh name again?"

"Karlei," I answered smiling shyly. I wish I was as bold as Beauty, and not as shy as I was.

"Oh, we don't have anything permanent as yet but you can come in Friday evening at 3:00 p.m. and we'll take it from there alright," then he continued after pausing briefly. "Have you ever done anything like this before?"

"Well just working at Burger King if that helps," I said jokingly.

"It's a little dif'rent than that, but you will learn," he continued reassuringly.

"Thank you very much Thomas, you will not be disappointed," I promised him as I shook his hand.

My feet could not carry me as fast as I wanted to walk. Anxiety flooded my soul. As I exited the restaurant, I thanked the Lord for everything, small or big that he blessed me with.

I could not wait to tell Doug the good news. Finally I would have some kind of independence.

By the time I reached home, Doug was home from work. I could smell that he had started to prepare dinner. Before I could close the door he was in the hall.

"Whey yuhh did deh, whey yuhh a come from?" >>>> (Where were you, where are you coming from?) He asked in his usual controlling voice. I had become very afraid of him. He had manipulated me into being scared of his tone and his controlling attitude. Fear immediately took residence inside my stomach.

"I went to Lilly's restaurant, Beauty got me a job, I mean she set up an interview for me today," I said softly as a child in trouble would have spoken.

"Yeah?" He replied sarcastically. "That's good," he continued then walked away without saying another word.

I began seeing things differently. Immediately. I knew somehow I would conquer all my fears and one day move out. For almost a month now I wished to go to college, but did not know how my tuition would be paid. With this job suddenly there was hope.

After I had gotten pregnant with Sulei, I had dropped out of high school, Prospect Heights High School in Brooklyn. Now I wished to go back to finish my education. I decided that if I got a job at Lilly's I would go back to school. I would first get my general equivalency degree (GED) and then an associate's degree.

CHAPTER 22

THE JOURNEY
Into Independence

My first day on the job was hectic. Thomas was right, working at Burger King was nothing compared to working at Lilly's. Everyone moved so fast. The waiters were good at carrying the trays on the palms of their hands. I was afraid of dropping all the food, so I carried it with both hands bracing against my stomach. Eventually, like everyone else, I was able to balance the tray with the palm of my hands. Eventually I was hired full time. Each day I worked from 3:00 p.m. to 11:00 p.m. I was very tired. But I was motivated because each day the customers gave us tips, which meant that I had money in my pocket every day, so I didn't have to depend on Doug for anything.

Two months later I went to Jamaica Satellite on Hillside Avenue for a month and got my GED. Immediately after, I registered at York College. I enrolled in two courses, Psychology and Sociology. It was difficult, but I was determined. I went as a non-matriculated student because I hadn't taken the college placement tests and I wanted to begin immediately.

My day became busy. After taking Sulei to school at 8:30 a.m., I went to York for my first class at 9:00. I stayed at school until 2:15 p.m. Then I went to work for 3:00. One of Sulei's friend's fathers picked her up from school and took her to the baby sitter. She stayed at the babysitter's home until I came from work at 11:30 p.m. Doug never offered to pick her up from the babysitter, not once. Instead, he would wait for me outside of the babysitter's home, and then we went inside to get her, together. I hated getting her that late because she was always sleeping. But I had to do what I had to do for us. Every day after work Doug asked whether I had met or seen one of his neighbors from Jamaica, 'Steven'. He said he came there frequently. Each day he asked the same questions, and each day I gave him the same answers. As always he annoyed me with his questions. Finally I asked one of the waitresses if she knew Steven, giving her the description that Doug had given me, gold teeth across the entire top of his teeth, medium built, and smiled a lot. She said yes. She promised she would let me know who it was the minute he walked in. That day finally came. And that day I was glad. Maybe now Steven would stop annoying me every single night about whether I had met Steven or not.

Steven was tall and average looking. His eyes were full and the most beautiful ones I had seen apart from Thomas'. When he smiled I saw that he had the top of his teeth covered in gold with his name inscribed on it. Something about him suddenly made me weak. I was attracted to him in every way without even talking to him.
I was tempted to ask him if he was Steven. There was something about his nature and character that fascinated me. Within five minutes of him sitting on the stool, drinking the soup he had ordered from the other waitress, I knew he was the total opposite of Doug. He was calm and his mannerism pleasant. He smiled often. Doug did not. And the glare in his eyes was inviting. The stare he gave was captivating as he carefully sipped his soup. Slowly. Slowly.

For a quick second I somehow imagined us together. But I could tell I was not his type of woman. Thoughts of us being together continued flooding my mind as the weakness in my knees heightened. I had never before believed in love at first sight. But this felt like it. There was no other explanation for my feelings.
I wanted his number, but did not know how to get it. I

would ask Raj. She was the only waitress that I had gotten close enough to, to tell her my inner feelings about anything pertaining to the job. She had briefed me in on the standards, and tricks and trade of being a waitress. I gathered enough courage to ask her to get his number.

After he left I felt empty, but I was no longer weak. I had acted stupidly the whole time he sat there. Perspiration had consumed my entire clothing from nervousness. But I was glad that he had left. Now I could go back to being me again, comfortably.

Each night after work, Raj and I took the bus home. As we headed for the bus stop, she bundled up her jacket. It was freezing outside.

As we made our way to the bus stop I couldn't help but to think of Steven every second, but my thoughts were quickly interrupted by Raj's complaining of the weather.

"This cold really getting to me," she complained; her Trinidadian accent evident.

"Mmm," I answered shaking from the cold. Tonight was unusually cold even though it was December.

"How come yuhh su quiet tonight?" Pausing she then add, "is di ugly bwoy Steven yuhh penny-ing?" >>>>
(Why are you so quiet tonight, is it the ugly boy Steven you're thinking about?)

"No," I lied, but then confessed, "I like him a lot, Raj."

"But you just see him one day and like him already?" Pausing again she added, "You're sick in your head?" She giggled.

That may have been true, but I knew I had to get to know him somehow.

The ride home was quiet. But I was glad; I daydreamed about Steven all the way home. Raj kept looking at me with a suspicious eye.

Should I even tell Doug I saw Steven?
I could not wait to tell him that I did.

Doug was at the bus stop waiting for me. He always waited. Before I could make it home he asked as expected.
"Suh, yuhh see him?" >>>> (Did you see him?)
"Who, Steven?" I asked nonchalantly, "yes," turning my face away from him as I blushed.
"Yuhh si him gold teeth?" >>>> (Did you see his gold teeth?) He asked mockingly.
I wanted to say 'yes I did, and you know what Doug I like them. I like him. I want him. I want to be with him and not you'. But I didn't. I couldn't. Steven didn't even know I existed. He didn't even care if I existed. He dressed in nice clothing with famous names written all over them. I dressed in whatever I liked that was cheap. But regardless, I liked him very much.

I nagged Raj everyday for the weeks that followed, until as she had promised, she got Steven's number. I called him several times. He was always busy and had little time to talk. He decided to pick me up after work one night so we could really talk. I was scared. I had never been in the presence of another man since Doug. What if Doug found out? He would definitely kill me. But I liked Steven too much to care what Doug thought or felt. I was torn between the decisions. Should I accept Steven's offer for him to pick me up or should I simply say no and keep it moving?
Eventually I became brave and accepted Steven's offer. The restaurant was unusually busy and the night could not finish quickly enough. I watched the clock on every hour. Finally it was eleven o'clock and time for me to leave. As I exited the door Steven tapped his horn softly. I was very afraid. I searched the streets with my eyes to see if Doug was anywhere near because if he was, I would lie that Raj asked him for a drive and I went with them so as not to stand by myself waiting for

the bus. But Doug was nowhere to be seen.
That night Steven took me and Raj home.

CHAPTER 23

THE JOURNEY
Towards The Future

Steven was everything I thought he would be. He was very calm and quiet. He seldom spoke. I had asked him if he could take Raj home too, and he said yes. He took Raj home first, then me.

For about two weeks he took us home every night. One night he shocked me by asking for a kiss just before I left his car. I was scared. If Doug found out he would kill me. I had explained to Steven that Doug and I were married. I had also told him I was with Doug just to get my green card. He hadn't seemed to care much. I even told him Doug had given me a description of him so I could see him to introduce myself to him. He had smiled slyly. He did not seem interested in me, or anything that I had to say. He just wanted a kiss.

So as I left his car I built up the courage and kissed him. His lips were soft and intriguing. As we kissed, his arms wrapped invitingly around me bringing me closer to him. I wanted to pull away, but something held us close. The tenderness of his arms holding my shoulders melted my inner being. My head became blurred and my entire body liquefied. My eyes remained closed throughout the entire kiss. His hold was strong enough to keep me there, but soft enough to entwine our souls. As I surrendered my being to his touch and kiss the thought of Doug coming back tomorrow evening flashed through my mind disturbing the moment of peace.

Doug had taken a trip to Jamaica. I was sure he was having an affair. But after meeting Steven the time he spent away didn't matter anymore. Before I would feel lonely whenever he left, but now I could not wait for him to leave since Steven and I had become friends. I now wished he traveled more often. I knew I would not have kissed Steven had Doug not been out of the country, so I

was glad he had left for the opportunity to feel the softness of Doug's lips that I had fantasized about. And just as they were in my fantasy, they were in reality – soft and moist and inviting. As I braced myself away from his embraced, he opened his eyes. In them I saw me. I saw a future together, a future of our defining moment when I would say I do. I wanted him for me. I wanted to spend the rest of my life in his embrace. Security and love were in those arms that I had just gotten lose from. The kinds I never knew, never felt. Then suddenly he pulled me to him again. Kissing him once more, I wished Steven to be the one I was going home to. And suddenly the shyness I felt before evaporated into thin air. Being on the streets of Queens in a car under a street light where we could be seen didn't matter anymore. And suddenly I wanted him more. But I knew I had to go. I had to get Sulei from the babysitter. I had already stayed past the time I normally picked her up.
As I left his car I knew somehow I would find the love I always desired in him.

Doug started traveling more often than normal. I suspected he was having an affair, but he denied everything. Sometimes after coming home from work, I would just not see him home. After asking his sister where he was that's when I'd found out he was in Jamaica. He often used the excuse that his mother was alone out there and he had to visit to make sure everything was okay. He became less interested in our relationship, if we even had one. He became less interested in me. He no longer cared where I wanted to go, or whom I spoke to on the phone. Although I was glad he had somewhat changed, I could not help but feel neglected. The change had come about too sudden and for the wrong reasons. I knew he was having an affair, even a child could see that. But I was afraid of his attention being elsewhere and not on helping me to get my green card as he had promised.

Steven and I became more entangled with each other, since he was a shoulder that I leaned on when I felt neglected. He was a source of escape. When I hurt, I would go to Steven. When Doug ignored me, I ran to Steven. Eventually all I wanted was Steven. The more Doug traveled, the closer I got to Steven. Soon, Steven began calling me at home whenever Doug was not around. But sometimes he called when Doug was home and I would pretend it was a wrong number. Eventually Doug found out that Steven was calling our home and everything started to fall apart more quickly. He suspected something, but I denied everything. Furthermore, it wasn't a lie. Steven and I were just friends. Nothing more. Yes we kissed, yes he held me as close as only a husband should, but that's as far as we went. So I really hadn't lied to Doug.

I got to know more of Steven's friends, who also knew Doug. They eventually told me the reason Doug went to Jamaica so frequently. That reason was Maxine. She was the girl who Doug was having an affair with. They told me the news without emotions while I sat in Steven's living room. I did not love Doug. But for some unknown reason, the pain was unbearable, but I managed to hide it. I had suspected his affair, but I never imagined it to be true. I did not want it to be true. But now it was. And she was pretty. They had said that too. That made things worse. I had wanted them to lie to me to tell me she was trash. Ugly. No good. What the hell would Doug want with 'THAT', but they had not. She was pretty and the hottest thing around. They said she had a cocoa cola bottle shape, sixteen year old breast, and the face of a goddess. My entire inside melted. My head suddenly felt light and dizzy.

I did not love Doug, but I had started to care. And even though I did not love him, the last thing I wanted to hear is that he was having an affair with a very pretty woman. I was confused. I knew I didn't love him, and I knew he wasn't my type. But the news of him cheating tormented me daily. Maybe it was the fact that I feared him changing his mind about helping me with my green card.

Things between Doug and I changed a lot. We constantly had arguments about the same topic – Steven. His suspicions grew about me and Steven. He became abusive with his words. He threatened to have Steven beat up by his 'boys'. He warned me continuously to stop hanging with Steven because 'something is going to happen', a warning that I never took seriously. I thought once again Doug did his usual thing – talk trash.

CHAPTER 24

THE ROBBERY

But Doug was serious. One night he had his friends robbed Steven. They used a girl to get his attention then pranced upon him like robbers. They took him into his house and gun whipped him.

Doug bragged about it many times. And so did his friends. They came by our house and bragged about it every day. They had threatened to use a curling iron plugged in to sodomize him. They said they had found marijuana in his home in a barrel in his room. They said they had thrown all his sneakers away on the highway as they left his home. I wanted to call the cops but I had no proof. And further more they had said they found marijuana in his home. Calling the cops could prove detrimental to Steven than to Doug. I despised Doug more than ever.

It wasn't a surprise that Steven no longer called. I didn't expect him to. He knew it was Doug. His friends knew it was Doug. I knew it was Doug. So I wasn't surprise that he chose not to call. I was completely empty without him. Weeks after weeks I listened for the phone to ring, but it never did. I realized Doug was nothing but a coward. I also realized that I had fallen in love with Steven and hadn't realized it.

Going to work was not the same. I looked forward to seeing Steven after work, but now there was no motivation. Now I just went to earn my money for college. The ride home from Steven had helped a lot. But now since he no longer came around, it took me forever to get home.

Sulei's friend's father, Jamel, still took her to the babysitter. He was a true blessing. He really helped us out. He not only took her to the babysitter, he made sure she had something to eat if I did not have the time to provide something for her.

He had moved here from Trinidad many years ago. He had sole custody of his son. His wife had divorced him and moved back to Trinidad. Jamel genuinely cared for Sulei and me. He always wanted us to be friends. But I was always too preoccupied with Steven on my mind. Jamel gave us everything that no one had ever given; he gave us genuine love as a friend. Unlike Steven, he never asked for a kiss. He never as much asked to touch my shoulders. He was much older than I was. On the weekend he would meet me at the park, our secret meeting place, and we would all go out together. His son was the same age as Sulei. We were like one big happy family. But soon after the joy, reality hit whenever I had to go home to Doug.
Doug did not like the picture of me and Jamel, and threatened to kill Jamel. I did not understand his motives, because he had his woman in Jamaica. But then that was Doug. I confided in Jamel about Doug and his violent temper. I confided in him about everything. Jamel kept asking me why I stayed. The truth was I promised myself that I would not leave without my green card. He owed me that much for all the pain I endured. But the real truth was I had a very low self esteem. I had to learn to validate myself without the presence of a man.
My friendship with Jamel grew as the months passed. Jamel helped me with the tuition for York College and gave me money for my books. He even suggested I take Sulei to Disney, all expenses paid. At first I was worried to take all that money from an almost stranger, but each time I saw Doug's face, I became convinced that I had to get away. I decided to go to Disney when Sulei's school was out during the summer. I told Doug about the trip. He insisted on accompanying us. But I refused to let him know when we the exact date was for us to leave. Fear of Doug getting upset took a hold of me throughout

the entire night, the night before we left. But I decided to go anyway. I needed a break from Doug. I needed a break from my fears. I needed a break from the struggles I faced at my young tender age.

CHAPTER 25

DISNEY WORLD

The flight to Florida took forever. Or so it seemed. Our only luggage was a carryon bag and Sulei's backpack. There was no checkpoint, so we walked straight from the airplane to a cab, which took us to the hotel where Jamel made reservation for us. He had given me all the directions that the travel agency had given him. The cab driver took one look at the paper after I handed it to him and knew exactly where I was going. Looking at me in his mirror he shook his head with approval.
"Vacationing?" his voice was deep and he seemed to have a cold.
"Ah, yes," I hesitated before answering trying not to sound nervous. But the truth was – I was nervous. I had never been anywhere this far by myself. The only time Sulei and I had traveled alone was to visit my ex-brother-in-law, Teddy, in Texas while we were living in Brooklyn before I had met Doug. Teddy loved Ilza, still. Although I was younger, I protected Ilza. So when Teddy tried to date Ilza I was livid. Teddy never gave up trying to be with Ilza. Even after he left Jamaica and came to America to live, Teddy sent money for Ilza, and an LP record with love music. Teddy would call Ilza almost every day. The letters he wrote to Ilza, we hid from my grandfather who would have killed Ilza if he knew.

My mind wandered back to the trip to Texas.

We had stayed there for a week just to get away from all the stress that was in our lives. Teddy sponsored the entire trip. We took the greyhound bus, which took us three days to arrive in Texas, three long gruesome days. Texas was very different from New York. It was more peaceful and serene. While in Texas, Teddy took me to a Club. I had so much fun. I didn't want to return to New York. But I had to. I didn't have a job, a green card, or money. I had nothing. So I couldn't possibly stay in Texas.

Now here we were again, but this time alone.
"Going to Disney?" he asked smiling excitingly.
"Yes," this time my voice crackled from the nervousness.
The cab pulled up to the curb of the hotel. As I paid him I wondered if I did right by telling him I was on vacation, alone.

Florida was beautiful. I decided that we would lounge around the hotel for the first day, to unwind, and that we did. Jamel had given us his American Express. I was shocked when he gave me his card only to see he had gotten an extra card with my name on it. I never owned a credit card before. This was my first. He told me to buy whatever Sulei needed.
Walking in the restaurant located on the ground floor of the hotel, I felt rich. I felt suddenly proud to be able to give Sulei another view of life different from the one she was accustomed to. She ate briskly away at the fries on her plate. She was a pretty girl. I was proud she was my daughter.

The next day we visited Epcot Center and Magic Kingdom. We saw Mickey and Minnie Mouse. We watched the parade. We went on all the kiddie rides. Sulei enjoyed our vacation. I called Jamel every day. I had wanted him and his son to come but he wanted us to have fun as we deserved.
We stayed in Florida for one week then returned to New York. I feared what Doug would say when we returned.

But I did not care because Sulei had fun, and I had gotten away from the stressful life with Doug.

CHAPTER 26
RETURNING TO HELL

The flight back seemed quicker than our flight to Florida. Maybe it appeared that way because I was not anxious to return home. Jamel waited for us at the airport. As I walked towards the exit, I could see his smile. He was so glad to see us. I appreciated Jamel's friendship a lot. Now seeing him I wanted to hold him, to hug him and thank him. But I couldn't get to that point as hard as I tried. I did not know how to hug. It seemed as if whenever I cared about someone, they always go away. Like Ilza did. Like my granddaddy did.

"Hey!" he hollered as if he thought I had not seen him.

"Hi," Sulei answered before I could, as she tugged on my skirt while pointing to Jamel.

"I see him," I replied while loosening my skirt from her grip, "Hi Jamel", I replied turning my attention to him.

"How are you doing?" he asked caringly

"Fine," she answered amidst her smile. She really liked Jamel. He was like a father she never had. He cared genuinely for us. We were lucky to have him in our lives as a true friend. At times I felt like I wanted much more, but I just could not. I couldn't take the chance, the risk, of messing up our good friendship.

He understood before I even spoke. He knew before he was even told. He cared before there was anything to care about. I just couldn't risk our friendship despite what my feelings told me. Despite his tempting stare. His caring nature, his gentle touch, or even the way he had held my face and kissed my cheek before we boarded the plane for Florida. I couldn't risk it at all.

"Did you call your husband?" I hated when he or anyone referred to Doug as 'my husband', even though he was. Disgust filled my bones and every hair on my head.

"No," I tried to sound as calm as my pretense would

allow. He seemed pleased that I had not, and I was pleased that he hadn't asked anything more about Doug. I did not want to deal with that part of my life, as least not just yet.

"Hungry?" he asked staring at me again with wanting in his eyes.

"For what?" I asked temptingly.

"I'm serious," he answered amidst his chuckle. He had a way of giggling that melted my soul.

"Okay, yes. McDonald's?"

With that he headed for Mickey D's. He had taken his son over to his mother's house for the weekend. As we headed for the restaurant, he held my hand. He had never held my hand before, but he dropped it immediately as he remembered that Sulei was sitting in the back of the car. Looking behind he mentioned that she was asleep. She must have fallen asleep as soon as she had sat down.

We decided to eat in the car instead of the restaurant, since she was sleeping.

"Lay her down on the seat. Here," handing me the blanket he retrieved from under his seat. It was his son's security blanket that he kept in his car.

"Thanks," I murmured as I took the blanket. I then lay her flat on the seat and covered her with the blanket, turning around just in time to see Jamel staring at my butt. I was so embarrassed. And so was he. Turning away, he drove to the drive-up window to order.

"What do….," but before he could ask me what I wanted to order, the girl at the window cut him off.

"Welcome to Mc Donald's, May I help you?" she shouted in the mike.

"One minute," then turning back to me he continued, "what would you li……."

But before he could finish, he was interrupted once more.

"Welcome to McDonald's, may......", she was not able to finish her greeting because Jamel cut her off.
"I said one minute right?!" he was upset.
"Oh, I'm sorry sir, take your time," she apologized.
"What do you and Sulei want?" he asked trying to gather his composure.
"Number seven for me," I answered glancing at the menu board, "and a chicken mcnugget happy meal for Sulei."
"Hello?" he shouted, but no one replied. "Hello?" turning away from the mike and facing me, he continued, "When they're supposed to be here, they're not...." But before he could continue she answered.
"Yes sir, I'm here," from her tone we knew she had been listening all along.
"A number seven, number two and a chicken mcnugget happy meal," he answered frustrated.
"What kind of drink with that sir?" she asked timidly.
"Orange."
"With all of them?" she asked softly but he ignored her.
"Sir is that orange with all of them?"
"Yes," I answered instead.
"Please drive to the second window," she replied sounding frustrated.
"They are so robotic," he said referring to the girl.
I had never before seen Jamel upset, but even when he was upset he was more mild mannered than Doug. Jamel got the food and then pulled to the side of the restaurant. Sulei was still asleep. She was exhausted. After eating Jamel decided to call it a day. I agreed. I too was exhausted. I just wanted to bathe and go to sleep. I prayed that Doug was not home. I prayed that he had gone to Jamaica.
We drove from McDonald's in silence. Occasionally he glanced at me, but I pretended not to see. I just needed some time to get myself in the frame of mind that would

be needed to deal with Doug's bull once I got home. Jamel slowly pulled up to the curb at our usual spot four blocks away from Doug's house.

"Wake up Sulei," she was still asleep. I had to wake her up because I knew I was unable to carry her in my arms for four blocks. Jamel had decided to stop four blocks away out of respect for Doug. And I had not wanted him to stop in front of Doug's house either so I was glad when he decided not to. I hated waking Sulei up from her sleep, but I had to.

"Wake up baby," I whispered before she finally she got up. I had wanted to hug Jamel, but my mind was no longer contented. I worried what Doug would say or do. He had suspected that Jamel sponsored the trip to Florida, but I had lied and said my uncle had sponsored us. I dreaded going home, but I had to, eventually.

As I walked through the door my heart raced uncontrollably. Doug was inside his sister's apartment. They were talking, but soon the talking stopped and I knew they heard us coming in.

"Where yuhh coming from?">>>> (**Where are you coming from?**") I could tell he was extremely upset. As he spoke he came closer to me.

"Doug! Behave yourself!" I answered stepping away from him. Just then his sister came out.

"Doug behave yourself nuh," she shouted >>>> (**Doug behave yourself**).

"She's disrespectful," he shouted back.

How could *he* accuse *anyone* of being disrespectful? All the times he had gone to Jamaica? Sometimes I didn't even know. And all the times he came home late, I did not even know where he was coming from, and never asked. And now *I'M* disrespectful. He had some nerve. I wish I had somewhere to go. But I didn't. So I knew I had to stay because I needed somewhere to stay. Somewhere secure for Sulei and me.

"Just leave me the hell alone and get out! Get out of my house!" I could tell he meant it.

He had said those words many, many times before. But I could tell he meant every one of them now. There was a time when I wanted to leave and he begged me to stay, many times before, more than once. But he would always beg me to stay, but now he wanted me out. I could definitely tell he was having an affair.

I would have let him come with us to Florida, but I just wanted to be by myself. He never suggested taking a vacation before. Not even to Coney Island. So I decided to take the vacation by myself. As he voice echoed through my mind repeatedly, I wanted to leave but I knew I could not leave. I had Sulei. Where would we go? I just could not leave. I could not be homeless with my daughter again.

Doug's behavior got worse to the point where he slapped my face. Eventually I called the police.

They came and arrested him because he had slapped my face so hard that my mouth started bleeding. I was scared that when he came out he would kill me, so I decided to leave before he came out.

CHAPTER 27

JOURNEYING... AGAIN!

That night I took all my things over my aunt Martha's home. Sulei and I slept on the floor in her hallway at nights. Martha lived in a one room in the basement of a house. There were two other occupants, both males from Africa. Sulei and I slept under a space under the stairs. I knew when either of the men came home, they would talk in their native language loudly.

The first night they knew Sulei and I slept on the floor in the hallway I knew they were surprised because they suddenly stopped speaking. I could tell they were surprised because I peeked at them the whole time they stood watching us lay there on the carpet that smelled damp. The hallway was dark so they could not see me peeking. But I saw the shadows of their bodies just stood there watching us. It came as no surprise then that a week later Sulei had chicken pox.

My future seemed dim, once more.
I had stopped working at the restaurant after coming back from Florida. I no longer went to school. I stopped communicating with Jamel, despite the fact that he tried desperately to communicate. Sulei and I once again had no home. No one to turn to. I had asked my mother once again to return home, but once again she had said no. I decided that I would never ask for her help ever again.

☆

Doug finally came out after spending two days in jail. He found out that I was staying at my aunt's house and came to visit two weeks later. He came almost every day begging us to come back home. I was surprised to

know he was actually begging us to go back to his house. I did not want to go back but I was tired of letting Sulei sleep on the floor.
Sulei had just gotten over the chicken pox and I wanted to give her stability once more. Whenever I looked at her, I felt pity for the life I gave her. I desired a more happy and contented life. But it didn't seem possible any time soon.
My mother had once told me amidst her anger that I would eventually live in a shelter. She had said that to me while I was staying with Sulei's godmother, and that was the only reason I went back to live with Doug. I fought hard to not let her words have any truth to it. It was the last place I expected to live with Sulei especially after she wished that for us.

A week later we moved back in with Doug. I hated him more than ever. And I resented his every touch. I got sick to my stomach just thinking of him being close to me. Jamel and I started communicating again, but not as before. Our friendship became distant. And I still had not heard whatever had become of Steven.

☆

Doug and his sister agreed to let their uncle, Mark move into their house. He would occupy the room next to the living room. He was a very humble man. He cooked and cleaned. Things changed after that. His uncle liked me, and I liked him. I guessed his age to be mid-sixties. He helped me maintain my sanity. He despised Doug and everything he stood for. Whenever Mark called Doug's mother in Jamaica, she would tell him about Doug and his many women. Mark confided in me, and told me everything. He hated everything about Doug and convinced me to leave him.

Hearing about Doug and his many women made me want to leave even more. I knew if Steven was around he would help me to get out. He was financially secure. And although Doug said Steven sold marijuana, I was not sure I could trust Doug's words. Or maybe I did not want to believe that.
Each day all I could think of was Steven. I missed him with all my heart. Whenever I traveled on the bus, I would always look to see if I saw him around. But never did. Months after months I yearned to see Steven. I became excited when I saw a car that resembled his, but got disappointed when the driver was someone else.

With Steven out of my life, emptiness grew inside me. A need to get to know God developed. There was a desire to know everything I could about the goodness of HIM. Tiffany had told me about a church that she attended while she lived at our house. She always invited me, but I never went.
I didn't have any clothes for church but I decided to wear whatever I had. I decided to go to church on Sunday, the same church Tiffany attended. The pain I was feeling was driving me to near insanity. I had no one to turn to. My mother refused me. My sister, Chez was too busy being in love. I had no friends. The only person I had was God and I had to get to know HIM.

CHAPTER 28

A Step Towards God

Eventually I visited the church. Throughout the service I searched for Tiffany. She was nowhere to be seen. After the service I asked one of the ushers for her. He said she now attended another church.
I was disappointed. I had come expecting to surprise her but I guess I'm the one who got the surprise. Doug had mocked me in the morning. He said my sins had gotten so many I was rushing to church to be delivered. He was right. That was the first smart thing he had ever said since the day I met him at my cousin's house. My sins **WERE** too many, and I did need deliverance.
I had started selling nickel bags of weed on the street corner of 37th Avenue and 99th Street in Corona. I needed money and I didn't have a job. A cousin in Brooklyn had given me quarter pound of weed on consignment. I worked it until I had enough money to buy my own. Soon I was buying a pound of weed at a time. I didn't want to be rich; I just needed money to support Sulei. So Doug was right; my sins had gotten so many, I did need deliverance. And even after deciding to go to church I still sold my nickel bags of weed. I knew God would understand even if Doug or no one else did.

The next day I called 3-1-1 and got the number to Tiffany's husband's workplace. I explained to him that I had visited the church, but was told Tiffany no longer attended there. He then gave me the number to where she worked.
I anxiously dialed the number.
"Hello," I recognized the voice. It was Tiffany.
"Hi Tiffany, it's me," I paused to hear her answer. Instead she screamed, "Oh my God! Karlei, you're alive?!"
I had found my best friend again.

I told her that I had visited the church I thought she still attended and they told me she no longer attended that church. I told her I remembered the name of the company Gary worked and called 3-1-1to get the number. I apologized for asking for her number. But she quickly shrugged the apology away. She was very happy to hear my voice. I was ecstatic!
We spoke for almost an hour. She told me of the church she now attended and told me it was a very good church. I decided to visit their prayer meeting on Wednesday, which was two days away.

The day to visit the church and to finally see my best friend finally came.
As I entered the YMCA where they held their meetings, two young ladies sat by the window talking. I felt uncomfortable and sinful. But I was glad to be in church.
I had gotten some weed from a cousin in Brooklyn and had stopped by 99th Street in Corona to sell it. I hadn't sold all and still had a few nickel bags in my pocket book. I also had my 38-revolver that I occasionally traveled with in my bag. But I intended to go to church. I didn't have the time to take them home so I took them to church with me. I was glad to be in church. But the fact that I had weed and a gun in my bag disturbed me somewhat.

As I entered the church I overhead one of the young women asked if the other had smelled something. I knew it was the weed I had just smoked before entering the YMCA where the church was held.

Shortly after I sat down, a middle-aged man walked in and greeted everyone. His name was Donald Ditson. His wife came in shortly afterwards. She seemed

younger, and was lighter in complexion. Her name was Joy. Soon after their three children entered. He introduced them also. Kenesha, Sharon, and Devina. It was hard to tell the older of the two girls, Kenesha and Sharon. I guessed Devina three or four years old.
I waited an hour before Tiffany walked in. She was surprised to see me. We had not seen each other for years. But she still looked the same. She hadn't changed. Her childish demeanor still remained the same. Her smile had not changed either. As she hugged me the tears built in my eyes. She was always like a big sister to me. Always filling the gap that was left empty after leaving Ilza in Jamaica.
After she and Gary had moved away from Doug's house, my life was never the same. I no longer had a friend to talk to. So I had turned to Steven, then to Jamel. But now I knew this is where I wanted to be.
I felt at home. A sudden feeling of belonging rushed inside my body. Finally I had come to the right place to know the right person. I knew I would find the Lord.
I enjoyed the service and promised to return to church on Sunday. A promise I intended to keep at all cost. I held my bag close to me throughout the entire service. Tiffany smelled the weed on my clothes and shook her head in disgust, but then came the smile and then she replied, "Only you!"

Tiffany had prophetically believed that I would eventually become a Christian. She had told me on many occasions that she should snap a picture of me in the clothes I wear so when I became a Christian she would show me who I use to be. I laughed each time she said it. Me, a Christian? Nah. I'm good was always my reply. Now here I was.

I did keep my promise. I went to church on Sunday and

got saved. I was baptized and filled with the Holy Ghost, the only way to heaven. After that, I went to church every Sunday. I started seeing Doug in a different light. I didn't want to be with him anymore. I decided to plan my way out of the relationship with Doug. I had confided in Tiffany about my real feelings for Doug. I told her the truth about the reason I was with Doug. That all I wanted was my green cared. She convinced me to stay. She said God honored every marriage regardless of the reason. Inside I knew I still intended to leave Doug. She convinced me to speak to our Pastor about the issue. He too tried to convince me to stay. But I was still determined to walk away from Doug. I decided to leave.
But no sooner than I decided to leave Doug, I found out that I was pregnant. I could not believe I had been so stupid. Doug's behavior got worst. It was apparent that Doug did not care much about the pregnancy. He still traveled to Jamaica twice per month and sometimes more frequent. He never gave me any money to help to buy things for the baby. I was broke. I no longer sold weed because I had given my life to Christ. He never once followed me to any of my prenatal appointments. I went through the pregnancy alone. Again. It was obvious that the love he once had for me was now gone.

For three months I suffered. Each day I was plagued by nausea. I couldn't stand to smell Doug's cologne. I wondered just how long I would suffer from the nauseating feelings. I longed to feel normal again. Sulei did most of the cleaning up. At eight years old I imposed on her playtime. She practically became my little helper.

My nauseating feelings finally disappeared the fourth month.

Doug had eventually agreed to sign the papers for me to start the process of filing for my green card. A year after I applied to the Immigration and Naturalization Services, I received my work permit and social security card. I was five months pregnant when I received my social security card.

Doug gave me hell while he was petitioning for me as his wife. Whenever he was upset he would shred the application forms and swear to never again sign them. Or he threatened not to go to the interview at the Immigration and Naturalization Service whenever they summoned us. Eventually he had signed the papers and I had sent them in the same day. Now here I was with a taste of freedom to work and provide for my children.

I decided to go back to work until the baby was born. I desperately needed the money. I contacted the temporary agency that I had worked for before. They sent me to the State Workers Compensation in Manhattan. Taking the train in the mornings was the hardest because I was pregnant. One morning on my way to the subway station, I met a woman, Alice. She was a Jehovah's Witness. Each morning she offered me one of their brochures. Every morning I refused. She persisted. Eventually I took one. On my way to work as I sat on the train, I decided to browse through the brochure. I was amazed. On the front of the cover it said "God **WILL** See You Through'. The article spoke of everything that I was going through at that time. Each morning Alice provided me with a brochure and each morning the title on the cover indicated what I went through either for that day or week. Things started looking brighter especially after my first paycheck.

CHAPTER 29

A STEP CLOSER

Sulei enjoyed going to church on Sundays. She enjoyed going *every single* Sunday. Doug saw the change in me and mocked me daily. I no longer depended on my own strength to carry me through. I now felt like I was able to move mountains and leap over valleys.

Six months into my pregnancy, Doug's cousin Mark confessed that Doug's mother had told him that Doug had gotten a girl pregnant in Jamaica. My heart was shattered. I never loved Doug, but I was hurt for some unknown reason. Maybe it was my hormones due to pregnancy. Suddenly I became MRs. Sensitive.

Now it all made sense – him going to Jamaica so often. Him not caring anymore. Him not caring enough. Or him not caring any at all to ask anything about the baby. Suddenly, it all started to make sense.
I confronted Doug about it and he denied it. But I knew the truth. I believed Mark. I may have been naïve before, but not anymore. Blind before, but not now. I now saw Doug for who he was, and who he would always be. His son's mother was right. I should have seen the signs. Maybe I had seen the signs but chose to ignore them because I knew I needed a place to stay and I knew I would never again subject Sulei to a life of hell like I had subjected her to before.

As my pregnancy progressed, I became more and more excited about it. All the dizziness had left. Sulei and I went shopping on the weekends for the baby. She was excited too. My due date was October 1st, and I decided to work until it became impossible. My stomach had gotten so huge. Sulei helped me in so many ways throughout my entire pregnancy. It was **OUR** baby.

Gloria, my coworker, with whom I was the closest to, planned a baby shower for me. After the shower, she offered to take me home but I refused. I refused because they thought Doug was the perfect husband. That was the image I portrayed. I was too embarrassed to let ANYONE know the truth! I had gotten together with Doug because I needed a place to stay and I needed my green card. I didn't want Doug. I didn't want the marriage. I wanted to leave Doug as soon as I got my green card.
But then I became a Christian and my best friend and pastor told me that God honored marriages regardless of the intentions. I had still decided to leave. But then I found out I was pregnant. Then I found out I was not the only one who was pregnant for Doug. So here I was stuck with a baby that *I* wanted.
Everyone at work thought Doug was a 'real' husband who loved me and was excited about the baby. I did not want to let them see the reality of my life.
As I thought of my life and what it had become I was choked up with tears. I had a normal life in Jamaica. Then I came to the land of milk and honey, and since then I suffered.
I had not done any wrong in life. So why was I suffering the way that I was? As a child I gave all my toys to other children. I held concerts for children in the community and provided food for them. My grandparents gave Ilza and me enough money for lunch to feed an army. So every day at school I bought lunches for other children whether they were a friend or not. I even held a party for my brother when I was only ten years old. I have not built a bridge or researched a cure for Cancer, but I did good things. So why was I

suffering the way that I was?

 I left work earlier than I normally did that day, and struggled home with all the gifts. I received a lot of gifts. I pitied myself as I struggled on the train with everything and my huge stomach.
Doug was not home when I arrived. I unpacked the gifts and threw them on the bed. I knew I was blessed because God provided. But the reality of my life was clearer now than it had ever been.

My mother also gave me a shower. Combined with the shower my mother gave, I had too much of everything.

It was obvious the love my mother did not have for me. During the baby shower one of her friends asked her to say a word of well wishes to me. I was shocked to hear my mother say she wished my pain will be far worse than the pain she felt when she delivered me. Her friend's eyes opened wide in shock. My mother made it seemed like a joke, but I could tell her friend did not find it funny, and neither did I. Her friend asked her what gift she would give me, and she once again had lied that her gift was too big to take to the shower and she would have it delivered to my house. I never received the gift. But months later I ran into her friend at an event and to hide the embarrassment I admitted receiving the gift that was never delivered.

My church decided to give me a baby shower also.
Six months after I started attending the church, I became a member. So they had tried their best to plan a shower, but were unable to. I did not attend church as regular as before because of the stress at home. The Ladies Department tried to contact me but was always

unsuccessful. I did not want to be reached. I just wanted to be left alone. Eventually they brought over all the gifts.

Looking at all the gifts I started singing the chorus, "How great is our God, how great is HIS name, HE's the greatest one, forever the same, HE rolled back the water from the mighty red sea, HE said I need you, put your trust in ME". I must have sung the song a hundred times as the tears kept flowing harder and harder.

I knew one day I would have the victory over all my trials. Over Doug. Over my mother's inadequate love for me. Over the lack of stability I gave Sulei. Over everything.

I knew one day I would be triumphant.

CHAPTER 30

FALSE ALARM

The weeks that led to October 1st took forever to come. I must have gone to the Emergency Room four or five times. But on all occasions they were false labor. On September 30th I woke up to the same nagging cramps in my stomach. This time however, they were lower towards my pelvic area. I called my mother to inquire about the cramps. I did not want to go to the Emergency Room again, only to be told it was false labor again.

On all four or five occasions when I had gone to the Emergency Room she had told me I was not in labor, but I had gone anyway. Now here I was calling her again, this time having more faith in her. I had come to accept my mother for who she was, and always will be, a friend. And that's it. She had birthed me, but she was not a mother to me. I had wanted more. I had wanted unconditional love. But maybe that was asking too much. Maybe she didn't know how to love. And even though she did not give me the love I had yearned for all these years, I loved her. There was nothing I would not have done to attain her love. But I came to the realization that she could not be convinced to do otherwise than her heart would allow. I finally confronted the reality that I would never know what it was like to have a mother's love. I would never know what it was like to lay my head on my mother's shoulder and cry. Or what it was like to hear her call and say 'I love you' before saying 'bye'. But I still loved her. And as that particular book says, when you can confront your pain that derives from the emptiness that lingers within, then you know the lingering of that emptiness will not dwell much longer. And finally I knew that indeed my emptiness had begun to subside.

"Hello?" her voice was rather low.
"Hello, are you okay?" I asked concerned.
"Yeh, it's just a headache," as she explained the reason she sounded low, her Jamaican accent slowly presented itself.
"Oh, I think I am going to have to go to the hospital today," I said choosing my words carefully. I felt embarrassed.
My mother and I never had that close kind of a relationship where I could tell her ANYTHING. We never spoke about condoms, or men, or sex. Those topics we deliberately avoided. Needless to say, this was also one of the most uncomfortable topics as well – having a baby.
"Oh, why do you say that, did you see some 'sign'?" she asked choosing *her* words carefully as well. I knew she meant if my 'water' had broke, or if I was bleeding.
"No, not yet," I said amidst the pain that shot across my lower abdomen. Bending over was the only way to relieve the pain.
Our conversation went on in the same manner, concluding with her telling me it could be the onset of labor. She called me constantly to see the progress of the labor pains. She timed them as well. She may not be the 'ideal' mother but she's always there for me when I needed her. She was there for me when I had Sulei and now she was here for me again. At times I wondered whether she was there for me out of love or out of loving to see me in pain.

After four hours of pain and cramps I decided to call a cab. The pain had increased and one of the signs my mother had asked about became obvious. I had arranged with the babysitter for Sulei to stay with her until I returned home from the hospital. My mother had to work so she was unable to care for Sulei while I was in the hospital. I had packed a bag for Sulei two weeks before when I had the false alarm.

The cab came quickly. I was afraid and nervous. But I knew it would be over soon. It would not last forever. It could not last forever. And I knew that God was with me all the way. Those thoughts helped me to keep my sanity. I could not believe I was going through yet another childbirth without a husband beside me. But here I was yet again.
Upon arrival at the hospital, I made my way to the 'Labor and Delivery Room'. A nurse showed me a room and told me to undress. She then monitored my contractions and dilation with a machine. The pain increased beyond belief. My back felt as though it was being torn opened. I *knew* I would die from the pain. I could not take the pain any longer. I kept calling on the name of 'Jesus'. Louder and louder. Just then one of the doctors came in and broke my 'water'. The pain escalated beyond the point of sanity.

CHAPTER 31

AND BABY MAKES 3

The pain became more intense. I knew it would be over soon, but I couldn't help but to think that this was hell on Earth. It seemed like forever for the baby to be born. Doug was nowhere around for support. Once again I was alone delivering a baby. My mother had been there when I had Sulei. But now she had to go to work. She promised that right after work, she would visit me.

The pain increased! And I just wanted to die. This continued for three hours. The doctors decided to do give me an epidural because my cervix was swollen and the baby would not be able to come through. Though it had dangerous side effects, such a paralysis, yet I agreed to the procedure. I was glad to not feel any more pain for an hour or two. They told me that the epidural would allow the contractions to relax enabling my cervix to relax, which would prevent further swelling of the cervix. They called in the anesthesiologist to perform the task. I was scared at first. But once it was over I was finally at peace.

I must have fallen asleep; because I was awaken by a midwife telling me that it was time to push. The baby was ready to be born. My cervix was no longer swollen. I began to push as hard as I could. The doctors and nurses coached me through it all. Finally my baby was here. I had a boy. His name was Nathaniel. He was my grandfather's namesake. At first sight, I fell in love with Nathaniel.

The setting of the room had helped a whole lot. Unlike the hospital where Sulei was born, this was more of a homely setting with a television and a phone already in the birthing room. I had a midwife available at all times.

There were also two doctors and a nurse. The room transformed from a birthing room to a regular room after the baby was delivered.

I had already known the sex of the baby after taking the sonogram, the nurse had told me it was a boy. Sulei had wanted a girl. He looked everything like Doug, or so I thought. He was very light in complexion, though Doug and I were much darker. But he resembled Doug so much. He was gorgeous though. But I guess every mother thinks the same. But he *was* gorgeous!

Sulei helped to choose the name for the baby. We decided to call him Nathaniel. That was my granddaddy's name also. Nathaniel and I stayed in the hospital for two days. Doug came to see him once and never came back. I lied to everyone who came to visit that Doug visited every morning. I was too embarrassed to admit the truth.

I was discharged two days later. I had no one to help me with my things into the cab awaiting downstairs. A stranger assisted me with taking Nathaniel and my things down the stairs to the cab as I left the hospital. The reality of Doug's coldness became clearer. He did not love us anymore. And he would never love us ever again. I felt completely weak inside. But I knew I had to be strong for Sulei and Nathaniel. I could not allow myself to break.

On my way home I had the cab stopped at the babysitter to get Sulei. She was so excited. I had called her every day. I missed her so much. I was so glad to be home, if even I could call it our 'home'.

Mark was glad to have us back home. Doug did not care. After he came home from work, he stayed in his sister's house instead. He no longer stayed in our apartment. He never held Nathaniel or even looked at him. One week later he took a quick glance at Nathaniel

and then left for work. The pain became unbearable. I knew I had to get out.
Taking Sulei to school was the most difficult task ever. I had gotten twelve stitches from tears I had received during delivery, so walking was the most uncomfortable and painful thing to do. My back still felt open from the epidural. In the mornings I had to wait until Mark came home to leave the baby with him and then walked slowly with Sulei to her school. Stopping every other block to rest because my back still felt open and sore.

Doug continued to ignore Nathaniel and me over the next year.

CHAPTER 32

A SACRIFICE OF PRAISE

I christened Nathaniel when he was a month old at our church. It was customary in Jamaica to christen your child early. Doug did not attend his christening. I went to my church and had the christening all by myself with Tiffany by my side. I had chosen her as Nathaniel's godmother. Embarrassment had enveloped my entire soul while my pastor performed the christening. As a Christian woman I stood at the Alter by myself without a husband. I was tempted to not have a public christening but I didn't allow my pride to hinder Nathaniel from being christened.

A year had come and gone so quickly. Doug was not present for Nathaniel's birth and he was not present for his first birthday either. His sister came, but he never came. And now the same shame that I felt at Nathaniel's christening once again took control of me at his first birthday party. I was too embarrassed to put my all into his party. No one knew of my shame, but it overshadowed me throughout the entire day.
That was the straw that broke the camel's back. I had to get away from Doug. I had to, and soon. I depended on my tax refund check to buy my furniture for my new apartment that I was soon to have if I intended to move out of Doug's house. I was afraid and excited at the same time. Sulei was very excited. Finally she would have her own room.

Eventually, Tiffany got me a job at Wonder Bread as a clerk for their outlet stores six months after Nathaniel was born. The pay was very good. I was able to afford clothes for Sulei. Now I would be able to change Nathaniel's diapers more frequently. Whenever he was wet I would delay changing him or kept him without pampers in the house. He only wore pampers when we had to leave the house. Otherwise, more often than not, he did not wear a pamper inside the house. Simple things such as buying toys for Sulei and Nathaniel would now be possible.

After filing tax I couldn't wait to get the check in the mail. Every day I waited anxiously for the mail to arrive. It seemed like forever waiting for it. Then one day it finally came. I decided to take the money and get an apartment and move away from Doug. This was the first time I was able to file for my income tax and I was excited.

My uncle, my mother's brother, had an apartment available on the second floor of his semi private house. My mother lived on the third floor. I was not sure if I was ready to live in such close proximity with her. But I had no other choice. I confronted him about renting the apartment. He was hesitant at first. He contemplated whether I could afford the rent or not. I finally convinced him to rent me the apartment.

Each apartment consisted of two bedrooms, a living room, a dining room, an eat-in kitchen, and a bathroom. That would be perfect for me, Sulei and Nathaniel. I started shopping for low-cost furniture. Since Doug and I had stopped communicating as husband and wife I had moved into Sulei's room. I bought a bedroom set for Nathaniel and me. Sulei already had hers. There were so many things that I needed, but I knew the Lord would provide. I bought a television and a VCR for Sulei. I bought a dining room set with a china cabinet, carpet, and a living room set, all with only $900.

Big Miracles, Small Packages

One day after Sulei came from school, we decided to walk on Liberty Avenue, which was close to Doug's house. The most popular furniture store was having a final sale. Today was the last day of his lease, which had expired and the landlord decided not to renew it. As we walk pass the store I looked in but did not stop because I knew his prices were ridiculously high.
"Hey," the voice was deep. A man stood at the entrance to the store beckoning us to him with his hand. He spoke little English.

"Mira, venaca, come," he continued, motioning me with his hand.
Walking towards him I started smiling. My money was not enough for his store but I went anyway.
"Yes?" I asked him curiously.
"I leave today. Everything got to go. Everything. The man no sign the lease no more." I guessed he was from one of the Spanish-speaking countries because of his accent.
Ignoring what he said I stepped passed him and entered the store. The furniture in his store was exceptionally fine. Italian pieces of furniture lined the walls of the store. It was clear to see he was moving, because the once orderly store now looked atrocious. Pieces of furniture were scattered throughout the store. As I looked in disbelief, I noticed a dining table with the matching china cabinet hutch, a piece of carpet remnant and a living room set.
"Excuse me sir, how much is this?" I asked pointing to the living room set, but before he could answer I continued, "and this, and this," referring to the carpet and the dining room set with its matching china cabinet hutch. I was like a child in a candy store.

"Oh they're expensive," he said twisting his eyebrows upward.
"I didn't ask you all that," I replied rather rude.
"Oh, all together, see expensive, ah, fifteen hundred. This and this worth that, but give me for all okay. Okay?" he said pointing to the dining room and the china cabinet.
"Fifteen hundred?" I asked astonished. I knew they were worth much more, but all I had was nine hundred dollars. I knew he would never agree. But it was worth trying.
"I only have nine hundred," I said shyly, but more embarrassingly. I couldn't even afford to buy the necessities of a house.
"Oh mammy, no. Can't do that mammy, you're killing me," glancing at them one more time, he continued, "I sorry. Can't."
Sulei had gotten excited, but now she frowned. I could tell she was disappointed. I wasn't disappointed though, because I didn't expect him to agree. I had only tried. That was the most I could do. Try.
Looking at my watch I knew I had overstayed my time outside. I had promised Mark to return within half an hour but now it was an hour later. He was babysitting Nathaniel. As I left the store I yelled 'thanks anyway'.
"We're not getting those?" she inquired with disappointment in her innocent eyes.
"No," I answered beneath my breath.
"Why?" she whined.
"I don't have the money."
Once again, I had disappointed her. I felt like such a bad mother. I could not even provide adequately for her or Nathaniel. Sighing deeply I felt a sudden sadness inside. Why did we have to go through so much Lord, why?
Halfway down the block, I heard someone shouting loudly as they could. "Hello, senorita!"
What now, I thought. As I walked towards him again I

started talking loudly enough for him to hear, "I don't have any money and I understand sir, that's okay."
"No, you can take them, I leave today though, you take today or no deal, okay?"
Looking at Sulei I couldn't believe my ears. It had to be the Lord. Only he could have made this possible.
"ALL of them?" I wasn't sure I had heard him correctly so I had to make sure.
"Si."
I could tell it hurt him to sell his furniture for what seemed to be below cost. But I wasn't disappointed and neither was Sulei.
"Okay, thank you sir."
My face could not contain its grin. After giving him the money, I left immediately to find a truck to move the furniture. I had no clue where to find a truck. Hurriedly I walked back to Doug's house to tell Mark the good news. He decided that he too would move right after I did. He despised Doug more than ever now. He despised Doug's mother too, and his sister. He was more anxious to move than I was. He decided that if he moved he would not let them know. He would move one day when no one was home.
"Hi Mark, sorry, I'm so sorry, but I found this store on Liberty Avenue that is going out of business, you know the real nice store?" I asked pointing in the direction of the store.
"Yes," he said nodding his head anxiously.
"Well, I got a whole lot of stuff for the apartment for nine hundred dollars."
"That's expensive man," he said frowning as he spoke.
"But you should see them, they're really nice." I then picked up Nathaniel who had fallen asleep and headed towards the door.
"Mek di wutless bwoy gwey," >>>> (**Leave the worthless boy alone**), he said referring to Doug. I could

tell he was upset. He only spoke that way when he could no longer hold his anger in.

I really liked Mark. He was a comfort to me when I really needed strength. I never really knew how he felt about me, but I liked him.

CHAPTER 33

A TASTE OF FREEDOM

I must have made six or more trips using a cab to move our things into our new apartment. I was so happy my uncle rented me the apartment. The truck that I rented had taken the furniture: our bedroom sets, and the furniture from the store. All that was left was our clothing. And I had decided to use a cab instead.

The day finally came for me to move. Doug did not care the least. A part of me wished he had cared somewhat. But the truth was he did not care anymore. As the cab drove off for the last time with the last of our clothing, I took one last look at the house I had called home for the past eight years. I had no help to unpack our things, so I did it slowly throughout the months that followed. I finally had peace.

Even months after we moved Doug still did not call. He did not even call to see if Nathaniel was still breathing. His sister called and so did Mark. But Doug never called. And when I called, he was never there. He now spent most of his time in Jamaica or hanging out on the streets with his friends. To Nathaniel and me, he no longer existed. To me, he had only been a sperm donor. To Nathaniel, he was a stranger.

My mother lived in the apartment above us. She apologized for everything she had ever done to me and blamed it on the cultures of Jamaica. She explained to me that she did not know how to deal with teenagers. I refused to believe that had anything to do with the treatment I received from her. Regardless of the past with my mother I now accepted her for who she was, a friend, and not who I wished her to be, a mother. At least that was my coping mechanism.

Things began getting better. Nathaniel was accepted into the day care center two blocks away from where we lived. Sulei attended a public school not far from our house either. Now all I desired was a car, which would make life easier for me when I took Sulei and Nathaniel to school. I had gotten my learner's permit when I lived at Doug's house. Now all I needed was a driver's license. I decided to take driving lessons. I did that for two months before deciding to go for the road test.

The morning of the test I was very nervous. I had the first appointment of the day. The man who sat in the passenger seat who would determine my fate seemed calm. I wondered how they trusted people like me to drive them. This was one job I wouldn't seek. New drivers? DEFINITELY NOT!

At the end of the road test he complimented me on my driving skills. On the paper he gave me he wrote, 'good driving skills'. I was overjoyed. My sister Chez had taken me to the site. She had used her husband's car. Chez had gotten married to Rick two years before I decided to move out of Doug's house. Rick had been the first boyfriend she ever had. They had a daughter, Denise, who was now three months old. I admired her stamina to remain in her marriage despite the many controversial issues she faced within her marriage. Rick and Chez had gone through much but she stuck with it because they both were in love with each other. He would bring roses for her each day and surprised her with boxes of chocolate and exotic gifts. I somehow wished that I could have that certain thing that Chez had. Maybe I would have been able to pursue the relationship with Doug. But I doubted it. Because the love that Chez felt for Rick, I did not feel it in the least for Doug.

Chez had influenced and convinced me to get my license. She had gotten hers six months before. She

could tell from the smile on my face that I passed the test. A wide smile decorated her face as I approached her.
"Yuhh pass?" >>> [Did you pass?] Chez inquired.
"Yep!" I said handing her the paper.
We both screamed together!
This was the first step to independence. At least for me it was.
As she drove me back home I expressed my desire to buy a car. She was glad I had come to realize what she had been telling me all along, that a car is a necessity especially when you have children. Now I was sure that I definitely wanted a car.

CHAPTER 34

WHERE THERE'S A WILL...

The search for a car was harder than I anticipated. I didn't have any credit. Therefore it was difficult getting a bank to finance the car. After searching for days, they finally found a bank to finance the car and I was approved. But the interest rate was extremely high because of the status of my credit – NONE. But I had no other choice.
I was approved for a small car – a Toyota Corolla. Even though it was small, it was fabulous. I did not have much driving experience but I knew I would have to learn, and quickly. Sulei was ecstatic. She wanted us to get a car. She had gotten tired of taking the bus to church, especially in the winter when we had to stand and wait in the cold for a bus to come. Now we had our own car and she was happy.
Having the car was truly a blessing. I was able to take Sulei and Nathaniel to school, shop at the grocery store, and run other errands more efficiently.

At first driving was very difficult. The drivers were very impatient. They honked and cursed. But I maintained my composure and didn't allow them to aggravate me. My driving skills eventually improved. Then I became the master of the streets. Sulei and Nathaniel enjoyed the luxury of a car because we no longer stayed home on the weekends. We frequented the mall instead.
Three months after I moved away from Doug, Steven called my mother's house searching for me. She said he had called many times before. He had asked for my number but she had refrained from giving it to him. Eventually, he called back but this time I answered the phone.
I had decided to visit her one evening. The truth was I didn't feel like cooking, so I decided to get food from

her. The phone had rung and she shouted from the bathroom for me to get the phone.

"Hello?" I paused, waiting for the caller to talk.

"Hello," it was Steven. Suddenly my knees became weak. Steven was all I ever wanted and needed. But after Doug had gotten him beat up on by his friends I had not heard anything else of him. He had always been on my mind. I had missed him *so* much. His kisses and his comforting hugs, I had missed them all. But he had somehow disappeared without a trace.

Before leaving Doug's house I prayed that the Lord would allow me to see him one more time. When it didn't happen, I had given up and moved on. But now here he was once again.

"Hi Steven," I managed to hide my eagerness.

"Hi, what are you doing over there?" He asked referring to my mother's house.

"I live downstairs on the 2nd floor, by myself," I deliberately added. I wanted him to know.

"What's the number?"

"718-XXX-XXXX. Call me back okay."

Before reaching down the stairs, I could hear the phone ringing. I quickly grabbed it up. "Hello?"

"Hi, Karlei what's up?"

"Nothing, where are you?" I missed him so much.

"California," he said cheerfully as usual.

"And you couldn't tell me?" A feeling of hurt overcame me.

"I know," he said in his usual apologetic voice.

Steven and I spoke for hours, everyday. He would call me three times or more at work. He kept asking me to visit him, but I refused. California seemed so far away. But he kept asking, and I kept refusing, until eventually I accepted. Steven had finally said the words I had always wanted to hear. He was in love with me and I was happy to hear those words. With Steven, words did not come easy. But when he spoke them, they were true. He never fabricated to satisfy anyone's ears, unlike Doug who lied often. Things that I use to sit and dream of doing with Steven or hearing him say were now reality.

CHAPTER 35

TOO CLOSE

Finding the Lord was the beginning of the dying of my emptiness. I felt totally satisfied and complete. The emptiness had dissolved and I no longer depended on anyone to make me feel whole. I desired to get to know the Lord more and more. I tried convincing Steven to get to know the Lord. The truth was I wanted Steven to get baptize, be filled with the Holy Ghost, and make me a good husband.
Steven came to New York on many occasions to visit me. We had such a wonderful relationship as friends. On one of his trips to New York, he gave me a ring, which he considered an engagement ring. I considered it a friendship ring because I was still married to Doug. I thought of a divorce, but didn't have the money to do so.

Steven had clarified all that needed to be clarified. He was not a drug dealer as Doug had stated. He fixed cars. He was not licensed as a mechanic, but he fixed cars. And now he had lost his job! It was the reason he had moved to California. The company downsized and he was laid off. He hoped to get another job soon after, but two months had passed and he was still unsuccessful in finding one.
Eight months later, he asked if he could come and stay with us until he found an apartment. I agreed. Steven in the same house with me!? I couldn't fathom. He was like my personal celebrity. I agreed anyway.

Occasionally Steven came to church with us. I loved him before, but I was getting to love him more. He was everything I dreamed of. That was until he started calling his friends that he had not seen after he had moved to California. That was until he started expecting more from me although I was a Christian. That was definitely before he started telling me I am going to backslide. And yes, before he started hanging out until 1:00 a.m. or later. I spoke to him constantly, but he didn't seem to care. He only cared about *'finding a job.'* At least that is what he said. But at 1:00 a.m. in the morning?!

Steven and I started drifting apart. I regretted allowing him to come into our house. Nathaniel had gotten attached to Steven. Now he would have to detach himself because I decided to tell Steven he had to go. Anything could happen to us when Steven came home at 1:00 a.m. in the morning. I couldn't subject us to harm. Furthermore, God had taken me from too far for me to give up now. . . So Steven had to go!

CHAPTER 36

RETURN OF THE DEAD

Doug started calling again. He demanded to see Nathaniel. After the way he treated Nathaniel now he was ***demanding*** to see him.

He finally admitted to having a girlfriend in Jamaica. She had broken it off with him. He described their break-up as being nasty and horrific. It was the same girl Steven and his friends had told me about. A satisfaction filled my entire being. Inside, I rejoiced. We started talking more often on the phone, especially when Steven did not come home early. Although Steven and I did not have a relationship, I could never let him know I was speaking to Doug. Not after what Doug and his friends did to him.

Doug and I reminisced. He apologized for everything he had put me through and I believed him. I wanted to believe him. I yearned for a family. I yearned to have a family like my mother had. I yearned to have a family like Chez had. I wanted my children to have a father figure. I wanted to have love. So I believed Doug for whatever it was worth. Doug and I started getting closer. I wanted that perfect image back again of a 'happy family'. The happy family I had before Doug changed. Before he started going to Jamaica. I yearned to be a 'family' again. I also yearned to give Sulei a 'father figure' in her life.

I had hoped that Steven would have come and filled that gap. But he had started to drift away with his friends. Steven had blamed everything on me. He claimed that he would have come home earlier if I did not quarrel so much, or 'wasn't so miserable'.

But how could I be different when talking to him was like talking to a door, or rather a wall, because at least a door opened sometimes. He opened none at all. He kept closed because I refused to give myself to him. I chose

Jesus and nothing would hinder me from remaining faithful to him, not Steven, not anyone.

There was a time I would have believed that the problem was with me, but not now. My emptiness was no longer there. And when I felt empty, I knew where to go. I knew I could go straight to the Lord on my knees. I no longer relied on my own strength to carry me through each day.

So nothing no one said would tear me down ever again, because the Lord built me back up. I no longer needed the comforting words or a touch from a man, because I knew where to find it now – from the Lord. And at nights when I wished I had someone to hold me, I just closed my eyes and I could see the everlasting arms of God wrapped about me. I wasn't wishing for Doug to come home because I was weak. I wished for him to come back to have a family. We were already married. We were already husband and wife. Going to church helped me tremendously because to me God always knew what I was going through and sent a word to alleviate my pain. And when my trials lasted too long, he helped me through day after day. So now I had nothing to prove to Steven because I no longer needed him to make me feel adequate as a woman. I no longer needed him to make me complete like I once did.

After he started staying out late at nights I realized I had the power in me to be strong and not allow myself to become weak once again. I had the strength to tell him to leave, and I did.

CHAPTER 37

ONCE BITTEN

Doug and I decided to try for "the kids' sake" one more time. It is pathetic how to excuse yourself from seeming extremely in need of love or remarkably desperate, how it becomes so easy to utilize the kids' presence to say 'oh I went back for the kids, you know'. But the truth was everyone around me was getting their life together, or had gotten their life together but mine remained literally empty. I decided then to totally dismantle the relationship I had with Steven.
Things between Steven and I had started to go sour months before I had made the decision to try again with Doug. I had tried to talk to Steven about his attitude and his coming home late, but he never changed. Steven and I had been through so many things together, but things were not working.
I asked Steven to leave and told him our friendship was not working partly because he had started coming home late. He would come home at 12 midnight, tired and not feeling to talk. I got weary of telling him night after night that if this continued, he would have to leave. It took me a while to build the courage needed to tell him to leave, but finally I did it. I told Steven he had to leave. I was frustrated and extremely unhappy.
Eventually he moved out.
After he moved out, he wanted to come back. He had gotten so desperate that he visited a psychic. The psychic had told him that someone was trying to separate us. What else would they have said, 'your life is perfect?' It was their job to take the negative and make it worst. How else would they get paid?
I had wanted Steven to come to church, accept the Lord as his Savior and then we would live 'happily ever after'. But it did not appear to be happening as I had planned and he kept dragging me down with him spiritually.

Because whenever he came home late we argued. And whenever we argued, I said things unbecoming of a Christian woman.

It never seized to amaze me how we as Christian women are so ambitious for the 'unsaved men' in our lives than we are for ourselves. We try to change these men into someone ambitious for the Lord more so than we try to change ourselves into strong Christian women for the Lord. But do they ever change? And if they do, will they marry us? And if they marry us, was it God's will? And if it was the will of the Lord, would we have had to put ourselves through the anguish and pain that we endured while waiting for these men to come into church?

So Doug and I decided that one more time we were going to put our all into our relationship.
He seemed to have changed a whole lot.
Everyday Doug brought groceries to prepare dinner for us. He called much less than he used to and questioned instead of accusing. But he still had a long way to go because sometimes his temper would flare at something I said that he thought wrong or did against his approval. I had become independent during the three years of separation. Doug's temper no longer intimidated me whatsoever.
I had found me and liked the person I found. The emptiness within had subsided and I no longer needed anyone's approval for me to be who I wanted to be. On any given day I could be just about anyone, whether you approved or not. And, if I decided to wear pink shoes with an orange skirt, so what? And if I thought that the sweater I wore made me look ten pounds heavier, and you thought the black suited me better. Today is my day, tomorrow yours, I will please you then, if I think you're worth it.
Two months into us trying to salvage what was left of

our relationship Doug decided to move in temporarily as a trial. I cleaned my house thoroughly. I lifted the bed, moved the dresser, the armoire, everything. The kitchen was meticulously cleaned and the bathroom. I changed my telephone number disabling my male associates from calling. This time around I was going to put my all into our relationship, making sure it worked. Coming home from work to a home cooked meal, my children, and Doug was enough to convince me to make needed changes. I wanted to restore 'the perfect family' image. But I couldn't help but feel like a fool.

Doug had just finished preparing dinner. As I sat with Nathaniel in my arms watching Oprah discussing 'Small Geniuses - Kids that Made a Difference Somewhere in the World', Doug called to say dinner was ready. He cooked, and I shared the dinner.
He then did something very strange. He went in my bedroom and locked the door.
Doug was always searching. Always snooping. Always looking for something to start something with.
As I approached the bedroom, I noticed he was laying face down on the bed. Curling beside him, I lay there in silence. Suddenly he turned around facing the ceiling. Then turned back around laying face down again. This time his head hung to the side of the bed closest to the wall. He fumbled with my shoes that I had neatly displayed against the wall.
"You have so much shoes, and all I have is 2 pairs," he said picking up my black shoes. Then he continued, "I could have more, but I not into those things. One pair is good enough for me."

Doug came to America when he was six years old but he still did not speak proper English. He did not have a pronounced Jamaican accent, but his English was unbecoming.

"Mmm," I replied in a low tone.

Then he stretched his hand farther underneath the bed.

"What the hell is this?" he asked coming up with a tissue that had a used condom in it.

I was in total shock. Where did that come from? I had cleaned underneath the bed. That was not there when I had lifted the bed. So where did that come from? Could Doug have put it there? Furthermore, I was sure Steven had not brought anyone in the house when I was not there. Or did he?

Getting off the bed he handed me the paper with the condom in it. Looking under the bed I saw another used condom. This was just not real. The strange thing about it is that Doug did not seem at all disturbed. He was somewhat hurt, but not angry.

Did Steven make love to a girl in the house when he was alone in the daytime when I went to work? Steven was many things but unclean he wasn't. He wouldn't have left a used condom under my bed. He was many things, but unclean was not one of them.

The day went on as usual. We ate in silence though. No one spoke except for Nathaniel. He performed his show as usual. Talking endlessly about nothing and everything. That night Doug and I had a long talk. He expressed his hurt and his disappointment. But somehow it all seemed too strange. Somehow I just did not believe anything he said. I still held on to the notion that he had placed them there.

Things between Doug and I changed drastically. I never trusted him again. The feeling of comfort started to vanish slowly. Doug started to stay over his mother's house more often, so I started seeing less of him. I was back to where I started, with no one. But this time the pain was not there and the attachment had been broken somehow. I was actually glad to see less of Doug.

After he claimed to have found the condoms, the feeling of trust had somehow died. I assumed that he intended for me to build hatred for Steven because of his negligence but it had all backfired. I was glad to be in charge of my house once again. And so was Sulei. She hated my entire decision from the start. She despised Doug's character and temperament. She totally despised Doug.

Doug called ever so often with sorry excuses why the relationship did not work. As if he thought I was depressed or in a deplorable state of mind because he left. Not this time. I could not subject myself to that trauma ever again.

I was glad Doug left. This time I decided to file a divorce immediately. I didn't want Doug. EVER!

Sometimes the Lord allowed a refresher course to remind you why you left the first time . . . and this was my refresher course. I earned an A!

CHAPTER 38

ON MY OWN AGAIN!

Being a single mom was not as I thought it would be. My divorce from Doug was finalized within six months. I had custody of Nathaniel. My day repeated itself each morning – took Nathaniel to the day care, took Sulei to school and then went to work. In the evening it was just the reverse.

I didn't have a life. Not that I didn't want one but I couldn't –not with two children. My mom lived in the apartment above me. But she only helped when it did not require much. In addition, I hated intruding on her for help.

The only other help I received came from Steven. After Doug had left Steven and I had started speaking again. I had stopped communicating with Steven because I knew that's what Doug had wanted. But now Doug was out of my life for good, I allowed Steven to call whenever he wanted to. However, I wouldn't make the mistake of having him live with us again. I would help him if he needed help but I would never make that mistake ever again.

As a matter of fact, I didn't want a man in my life. At least no time soon. I was fine the way I was. My kids and I! My mother joked many times that as a young lady I should be seeing someone, and questioned if all was well with me. All was well with me, that is why I needed no one.

CHAPTER 39

TWICE SHY!

"Let's go Nathaniel, please hurry, Mommy gonna be late for work," I was never early for work. No matter how early I got up. Furthermore I went to bed extremely late. I had the computer fixed at the store I bought it from, and now it worked perfectly well. I had gotten a trial compact disc (CD) for 500 hours of Internet service and was online for hours. Being new online was an adventure that I enjoyed.
It was difficult getting out of bed this morning and I wished to remain asleep. But reality came with my daughter repeatedly telling me to get up. She hated going to school late especially on Mondays.
I got Nathaniel dressed. I forgot that I had parked the car across the street the night before. I was unable to park in front of the apartment before 7:00 p.m. After I came back home with the computer, I decided not to wait until 7:00 p.m. Now I would have to cross the busy boulevard to get to the car.
"Let's go people," I shouted once more before putting on Nathaniel's jacket while I headed for the door.
"Sulei, let's go I said," shouting even louder.
"Okay, okay, I'm coming," she said in the usual voice she used whenever she felt she was being annoyed.
"Excuse me?!" I asked. Giving her my usual look that told her to take a step back and recognize that though I might be a young mother nevertheless I am a mother. As usual her apologetic stare told me she knew what time it was. She knew the deal as to what I was saying without me even saying a word.

I decided to wait for Sulei outside. I stood by the door and stared across the street to where I had parked the car. My car was not there! Just the space where I had left it stared back at me. My mind was left baffled. I had

locked the care with the multi-lock just before setting the alarm. So where could it have disappeared to? Grabbing a hold of Nathaniel, I ran back inside.
"I'm coming. I was just coming down," Sulei said stepping aside. From her body language I could tell she thought I was angry because she took so long.
"My car is not there! I don't see my car!" I said ignoring what she had said. She then realized that I was not coming to her, causing her expression to change.

The front door slammed. It was my stepfather. I could hear his footsteps pounding against the steps as he walked up the stairs. He had taken my mother to work an hour before.
"Did you see my car outside this morning when you left?" I asked with hope.
"No, I wasn't even paying attention, where did you leave it?" his asked, his face showing concern.
"Across the street," I pointed, as though he could see through the wall.
"Are you sure?" he questioned.
"Yes," I answered frustrated.
I did not know where to begin. I did not know whom to call. I explained to Sulei that I thought someone stole the car and that I would be walking Nathaniel to school. But that I would ask my mother if my stepfather could take her to school whenever he took my brother, Daniel, and my smallest sister, Kelly to school.

My mother had Kelly two years after I had Sulei. Kelly was spunky in every way and aged beyond her years in attitude. I guess that's from being the youngest.

My thoughts drifted back to my car. Who should I call first?
After Doug and I decided that it would not work between

us, I had started to speak to Steven again. I would sometimes see him at lunch. Whenever he came he brought me lunch. Steven and I still had a lot to talk over. One thing for sure, I was not going to allow him to move back in with us.
I decided to call Steven first, instead of the police. He would tell me who to call first and exactly what to do. He always knew what to do.
"Hi Steven?" I said immediately as the person picked up the phone.
"Yes, what's up?"
Despite our differences, he was there whenever I needed a shoulder to cry on. Nothing ever dissuaded him from being a true friend to me. Even after he had moved to California, he had wanted me to visit him. I had refused his offer.
As a store clerk for Wonder Bread I traveled to different stores, wherever I was needed. Steven had bought me a cell phone and a beeper just to keep in touch with me. He was always a friend. Steven had gone through many traumatic situations because of Doug. Yet, he never aborted our friendship. He always remained a true friend. But I had given up on us. Steven had made me feel totally complete in the beginning but that soon turned sour after he moved in and started staying out late at nights. And though we were only friends, I thought it very disrespectful.
Here I was embracing his friendship again, but this time I knew it would not be as before.
Steven had really loved and cared for me, but he had taken advantage of my kindness towards him. I could have been more understanding but I chose not to understand because I felt he was very disrespectful. He never helped with the bills while he stayed at our house. He never helped to buy food. Yet he had breakfast, lunch, and dinner. He never bought gas for the car. Yet,

every day he drove my car. The least he could have done was to respect my house and not come in at 12 p.m. or 1:00 a.m.

I admired many things about Steven. The one thing I admired the most was his forgiving nature. Nothing that was done to him he took personal. He hurt, but he knew how to move on. He knew how to look beyond someone's fault and see true character. And even though I had literally kicked him out of my apartment, he would still be there for me if he could. I knew I could depend on him. I guess that's why I called him first.

As I fumbled for the right words to ask, I couldn't help but regret having gone back to Doug. A deep sense of hurt ran through my body causing the bones in the palm of my hands to ache.

"Well, what is it?" he asked again, but this time impatiently.

"They stole my car," I had tried being brave until now. Tears formed within my eyes. I had tried to be brave because Sulei and Nathaniel were still at home. But now that I was alone, I allowed the tears to flow.

"Yeah right," he said as though he thought I was actually joking.

"I'm serious."

"From where?" he said appalled.

"Across the street. You know where the car dealer is? Right there."

A year ago a car dealer had moved right across the street from where I lived.

"Didn't you put the lock on the gear stick?" he asked trying to understand how it had been possible.

"Sure."

"Are you sure?" he repeated.

"Of course," I replied.

"What about the alarm?" he asked.

"It was on. I remembered it was on because I took the

computer to fix, when I returned back home I put the computer on top of the car, went back in the car and put on the lock, then I set the alarm," pausing for a moment before continuing, "so I know I put it on."
"Did you call the police?"
"Not yet," I didn't know just where to begin. I was totally confused. Suddenly I did not know myself anymore. I could not see myself without a car now. I needed a car to get to work. I didn't know how I would get to work. Going to Long Island from Queens was surely a long ride on the train. I did not know just where to begin.
Work! I had forgotten. It was now 8:39 and I hadn't called my supervisor yet.
"Listen, I'm going to call my job, I'll call you right back."
"Okay."
My supervisor was not there so I spoke with the supervisor of the other department. She was dumbfounded. The sympathy she gave brought me near tears.
I then called Steven.
"Yeah," I could tell he had gone back to sleep.
"Steven?" I wanted to ask him to take me to the police station, but I did not know just how. My pride hindered me.
"What is it?" he was always straightforward in everything. The way he answered told me he knew I needed his help and he waited for me to ask for his help.
"Can you take me to the police station?" the words finally came rolling off my tongue.
"Sure." He was always ready to help.
"Thanks Steven."
But he never responded. Instead he hung up the phone. I wondered if he would come for real or if he was playing games as he sometimes did. But he did come.

CHAPTER 40

IN SEARCH OF A COROLLA

Steven took me to the precinct to file a report. But I was not allowed to do so. I was told that I had to call the police from my house and the report had to be taken from the site of theft.

So Steven took me back home and waited outside in his car. The ride to and from the precinct was quiet. He never spoke and I never said a word. My mind was filled with too many things that were going on in my life to be bothered with anything else. I somehow wished it all a dream. As soon as I reached inside the house I called the police.

It seemed like forever before they came. I assisted in filling out the two pages of the report, which helped to make the process faster. After they had left, I invited Steven inside. He had not slept much the night before, so as soon as he sat in the living room he fell asleep. He had complained of a toothache that had kept him awake.

I spent the entire day making reports and contacting the insurance company. I never knew having a car stolen was so hectic. The representative for the claims division of my insurance company asked me questions that made me feel as though I stole my own car. The whole incident left me extremely stressed and exhausted.

Sulei came home from school at 3:15 p.m. We both sat in the living room watching television, while Steven slept.

I then called Doug's job to let him know about the theft of my car but he was not available. The man who answered said he would give him the message as soon as he saw him. I was uncomfortable having Steven inside my house. Eventually he got up, washed his face and left. I was relieved. I did not enjoy Steven's company so up close and personal any more. I think maybe because of what Doug had done to him before. I was afraid if he

knew Steven came by my house, he would let his friends beat him up again. Doug was very evil. And the more I thought of his evil ways, the more I questioned myself why did I rekindle our relationship? The truth was I had wanted companionship and a family.
Sometimes we as women get so desperate we settle for anything called 'man'. Even if it's an alien with a man's head. We'll sometimes settle.

The next day Doug called. After telling him what had happened he somehow did not seem appalled. He gave off no form of sympathy. Instead he immediately accused Steven of having my car stolen. I was left in awe of his accusation. I couldn't help but wonder if Doug had gotten my car stolen. As the minutes passed I became more convinced that he had gotten my car stolen.

CHAPTER 41

THE DEVIL HAD A TRAP SET

After my car was stolen, Steven took me to work daily.
He was always on time.
But this morning he was late. I had been calling Steven all morning but he was not answering his phone.
Looking at my watch I realized that he was late. Pacing the floor in my living room I became anxious. Sulei had just gone upstairs to my mother's house. My stepfather agreed to take her to school in the mornings when he took my youngest brother and sister to school. The only part of my stepfather taking my daughter to school was the fact that instead of driving her to her school which was a block and a half away, he dropped her off on the main street. She then had to walk to school. I never understood why he did chose not to take her all the way.

I had already taken Nathaniel to school. Now I waited anxiously for Steven to come to take me to work. He was late. I knew he was on his way because he never broke his promises. Suddenly the doorbell rang, that had to be him. Grabbing my bag I quickly opened the door to meet him downstairs.
"Hi you're late," but after greeting him, I realized something was wrong. "What's the matter, are you okay?"
He looked pale.
"My stomach again," he answered holding on to the door.
"Come upstairs a minute, let me make you a cup of tea," I said turning back upstairs.
Once inside I called my job to let them know I would be late. Heading for the kitchen I couldn't help but feel the pain he felt from the growling sounds he made. He was bent over on the chair against the wall from the pain in

his stomach. He then moved from sitting in the chair and knelt on the carpet with his head on the chair instead, crippled from the pain. I quickly made the tea and brought it to him.
The front door to my apartment suddenly opened. It was my mother.
"Little girl, you didn't hear me knocking?" she asked in her usual authoritative voice. She always liked to think she had control, and I fed her womanly ego.
"Steven is sick, his stomach hurts," I said looking at him still doubled over in pain.
"He need tea?" she asked. She always liked Steven. She said he was very respectful.
"No, I just gave him some."
"Oh." But before she could finish her statement the doorbell rang.
"Who is that ringing my bell this early in the morning?" My mother hated people ringing the doorbell so early. She did not care whether they rang her bell or mine. Heading towards my kitchen, she went to the intercom on the wall directly over the microwave.
"Yes?" she asked rudely.
"It's the police."
"Police? We didn't call you. Maybe you have the wrong address."
"Is this 109 Northern Blvd?" From the manner in which the police spoke I knew he was reading the information.
"Yes. But no one called you."
"Ma'am can you come down for a minute?"
"Sure," she answered him then returned to us in the living room, mumbling she didn't know what they wanted from her.
Steven had gotten up and was now sitting on the chair. I followed after my mother as she headed down the stairs. Before I left I could see a sense of concern on Steven's face.

Sulei must have heard the bell because soon after she came downstairs to join us.

"Can you believe these people?" my mother complained referring to the police.

We both went down the stairs to speak to the police. As she opened the door, the cops walked in.

"We had a report that there was a disturbance on the second floor," he said looking down on the paper he held in his hand. There were three other officers standing in the doorway behind him.

"Sir, I think you have the wrong address," my mother insisted.

"No ma'am, this is the address we were given."

By this time my stepfather had come down the stairs too and was standing directly behind my mother.

"Well, it's just me and my husband and my kids. This is my daughter," she said referring to me then continued, "and she lives on the second floor with her two kids and I live on the third. But if you would like to come up and see for yourself…" she continued as she moved herself out of the way to allow them to pass.

"Sure, thank you," the cop in the front replied as they all made their way upstairs behind her. The sound of their boots against the stairs sounded like the hooves of horses. They all looked around the house to observe for signs of disturbance. Satisfied, they left.

I found it strange, but I said nothing. I wondered if Doug had called them and made a false report. But I flung the thought to the back of my mind. Why would he do that? What would be the purpose in him doing that?

CHAPTER 42

THE CHASE

After the cops left, five or ten minutes afterwards, my mother left for work and so did everyone else in the house except for Steven and me.

"Listen hurry and put on your clothes so that I could leave." By the tone of Steven's voice I could tell he too was suspicious.

Hastily I put on my clothes and we departed. By the time I was finished getting dressed, Steven had left the apartment. He was sitting in the passenger seat when I reached outside. As I got in the car I fixed the side and rear view mirrors and adjusted the seat.

"Still feel sick?" I asked just before moving off. But he did not respond, instead he made a growling sound from his pain.

As we entered the Grand Central Parkway he told me to look in the rear view mirror to see if I was being followed. I thought he was just being paranoid. But that's when I knew he too was thinking the same way I was. That Doug had something to do with the cops coming to the house this morning.

Looking in the rear view mirror I saw nothing suspicious and sighed deeply. Waiting to enter the flow of the oncoming traffic, I moved cautiously towards the middle lane.

Suddenly there was a hard bang on Steven's car. Shocked, I looked in the rear view mirror. It was Doug. He banged his car against ours three more times. Fear took hold of all the courage that I had inside. I suddenly felt weak and my head felt dizzy.

As I moved to the left lane, he remained to our right. I was relieved. I thought now he would have left us alone. But I was wrong. Speeding up to our car, he looked at Steven and then at me with hate in his eyes. All the cars around us on the highway stayed at a distance from our car.

Doug's car was ahead of ours. He had moved in front of us. Then he moved to the right lane and slowed down. Suddenly he stopped his car again beside ours, called me a B----, and then slammed his car in the right side of our car causing it to spin half way around twice. Then our car spun once to the left, then to the right again. Steven held onto the steering wheel trying to help me to keep full control of the vehicle.

"Watch out Karlei, he's stopping for you to run into the back of his car!!!" Steven screamed.

Swerving out of his way, I stepped on the gas and tried to drive as fast as I could. But he still kept coming towards us.

"Call the cops Steven, call the cops!!!" I screamed.

"Hello!? There is a man chasing this lady on the Grand Central."

As he spoke I could tell that fear had taken a hold of him as well.

"Tell them he's stalking me!!" I screamed.

"I think he's stalking her," Steven continued giving information to the person on the phone.

Doug still kept coming at us. As he approached the car, I tried getting his license plate number, "Tell them his license plate number is xxx3301!!"

As Steven repeated it, I was angry that once again I had endangered him one more time. There was no reason behind all of this. Absolutely no reason. Doug and I had tried to reconcile our marriage one more time, but we both had come to the conclusion that it was not working. We had both outgrown each other. If we were even together in the first place, because I had gotten together with Doug at first for a place to stay. Then it was because I needed my green card. Why would I then try to be with him for any other reason? I had matured and desired a family and I thought since I was already married to Doug we could make it happened. But it never played out that way and things could never be the same for us ever again.

The things that I had admired in Doug were not admirable to me anymore. I doubt if I had even admired ANYTHING about him at all. All I had wanted was a place to call home for Sulei and he provided that. Furthermore, the way I use to be – insecure, empty, and searching for something to fulfill that emptiness, I was no longer that person. I had found the Lord on a Sunday morning in a YMCA we called church. I had found something sweet and fulfilling.

I had found something that gave me peace even when there was a downcast of storm surrounding me. Something that made me smile even though tears came rolling down. Something that when there was yet no one around, I felt loved. Cared for. Wanted. Needed. Something that placed a bubbling kind of feeling way down deep. A certain something that though I do not know what tomorrow holds I was hopeful for tomorrow. Something that took away all fears of evil. I had found the sweet beautiful aroma of God's presence. Of knowing that regardless of my faults, or if tomorrow I woke up without a husband, or a friend, that someone was there no matter what.

So I was not the same. Couldn't be the same.

And Doug found that hard to deal with. And I too found him hard to deal with. So we had come to a decision to be friends while we still had a good open communication for Nathaniel's sake. For whatever it was worth, because Doug's communication skills were like that of a two-year old.

Have you ever wondered how on earth you got with a certain person after the relationship has ended? Doug was the epitome of 'a wrong excuse for a man'.

As I looked back at Doug's car getting closer and closer, I sensed the fear of death within me. Steven was calm, unlike me who nervously drove his car amidst the heavy traffic on this Monday morning on Grand Central Parkway. Doug had death in his eyes and revenge on the wheels of his car. I made my way to the Van Wyck Expressway with Doug in pursuit. He continued chasing us still as we headed towards the Belt Parkway. I was tired and fearful all at the same time. I could not go on any more. I was weary from all the driving and the hitting of his car on ours.

Steven advised me to exit so he could drive instead. I preferred him driving because he was a much better driver than I was. Exiting off the Belt Parkway was difficult because there were so many cars on the road. But eventually I did it, and furthermore I was a new driver.

As I made my way down 182nd Street, off the South Conduit, I looked to see if Doug was still pursuing us. He was nowhere in sight. So I pulled over. I quickly got out of the car, but then procrastinated from the shock of it all. Suddenly there was the sound of tires over the asphalt of the street. It was Doug's car. He had found us. He kept coming at full speed. I thought he would slow down. But instead he slammed his car into Steven's. The entire left side of the back of Steven's car crashed in. Without warning Doug exited his car and made his way to where I was. As he approached me I stepped back. He continued to move towards me and then slapped my face. Astonished, I slapped him back. I was prepared to fight with him on the streets of Queens. My instinct reached in my bag but I suddenly remembered the 38 revolver no longer held its residence there. I was now saved. For the first time I regretted being saved and not having my steele piece as protection. I envisioned me holding against his temple, pushing him against the wall, forcing him to sit, and busting both knee caps out. But then I remembered I was saved and sanctified and this too was a trial that would pass.

Doug made his way to the other side of the street and picked up a white piece of pipe and ran towards Steven's car. Steven must have seen Doug coming because he stepped as hard as he could on the gas and left. Doug jumped back in his car and chased Steven again.
I was left standing in the middle of the road, confused. I had never seen Doug this evil before. I worried for Steven. As I stood in the middle of the street wondering where to go, I looked towards the highway for some sign of hope. Suddenly I heard the voice of a man calling.
"Need help? Want me to call the police?"
It was an elderly man standing at his gate. He had seen everything.
"Who was that?" he asked concerned.
"My ex, trying to kill me and my friend." I was still in total shock as I tried to gather my composure.
He took me into his house where his wife had been waiting for him to return. She welcomed me in and then called the police. Her husband took the phone from her and explained what had happened.
He was much taller than his wife. She was petite and beautiful. He weighed about two hundred pounds. They had pictures of their children all over the house. On the center table were two pictures of two children with uniforms on. They apparently were in the armed forces. I asked the woman permission to call my job to let them know what had happened. My supervisor answered, but I was unable to speak. I was suddenly overwhelmed with fright and started crying, so she was unable to

understand anything I said. She told me it was okay, to gather my composure, and to call her back.

CHAPTER 43

SOMEBODY CALL 9-1-1

The cops came within minutes of the call. They took the report but couldn't take an accident report because there was no evidence of an accident. Steven had left because Doug continued the chase. So instead they did a report for harassment.

I had tried calling Steven on his cell phone. After a third attempt, he answered. He gave me his location. I asked the cops to take me to where he was so I could get my pocket book out of his car. They agreed. I had not gotten a chance to get my pocket book before Doug had slammed into Steven's car.

I thanked the elderly couple and then left with the cops to find Steven.

Upon arrival at the location where Steven told me he was, I saw an ambulance and a cop's car. I also saw Steven's and Doug's cars. As I exited the police car I walked cautiously towards the other police car that was parked directly behind Doug's car. The police officers who had taken me there exited the car too and went to talk to the other cops on the scene. As they neared the car I stepped back and waited for them to finish talking to the cops on the scene. They took forever or so it seemed. I decided to walk back to the car. As I walked towards them I could see the look of disbelief on the policewoman's face.

"Come here this," she said beckoning her partner. "This is his wife."

I read her lips and knew what she was saying even though she had whispered to her partner.

"That's not true!" I shouted.

"Miss, you have to speak to them," she said brushing me off with her hands and quickly vanishing in her car. They drove off immediately. I suddenly felt cheap and

ashamed by what the cop had chosen to believe. I had wanted to tell them the truth. The truth about Doug. That he had lied.
Yes we were married, but I was not his *wife* anymore. I had only been his wife on a piece of paper. I had wanted them to believe me. But they chose to believe otherwise. I couldn't believe the stupidity of that black woman representing herself as an African American woman. I thought the law was supposed to hear both sides of the story before coming to a conclusion. But as it showed she loved drama. She thought this drama and ran with the story. I only imagined the conversations she shared with her girls later that night of what Doug had told them.

I slowly walked over to the other police car that waited. I bent my body low enough at the window to see their faces.
"Excuse me, what did Doug tell you? Who's in the ambulance?" I was shaking all over. I just wanted to make sure Steven was not in the ambulance. If it was Doug then I didn't care. This all seemed like a nightmare. But it was not. I had somehow wished that I would suddenly open my eyes and found out that this was just a bad dream. But the reality of it stared in my face as I looked at Doug's and Steven's cars parked in front of me. Steven must have gotten out of his car and was around somewhere.
"Well, he said he's your husband, and he came and found you and this guy in bed."
My mouth fell open. What?! Why was Doug doing this to me? How could he even lie to the cops of all people? Yes, I have lied before. But this was just ridiculous.
The police continued, "He claimed your boyfriend pulled out a gun at him and then when he picked up the phone to call the cops, you both ran downstairs and he chased

you both. He said he was coming from a hard day's work."

I was in shock. Doug had lied pathetically and I could not believe it. I asked the officers if I could tell them what really happened. I was overjoyed to hear them say yes.

It all made sense now – my car being stolen and the cops coming to our house earlier that morning, and Steven telling me to watch if someone was following me. It all made perfect sense. Every bit of everything that had happened Doug had planned it all.
On the Grand Central he had blocked our car with his and had gotten out. He had then jumped on the hood of our car. He had mentioned that he had already reported us to the police so he could do whatever he wanted to us. He then used his foot to kick the windshield. When it didn't break, he jumped down and punched the window of the driver's side. That's when Steven had told me to drive off. As I drove away he once again punched the back window in his final attempt to break the window. Then the pursuit had started all over again. It all made sense. I just was not sure what he had told the police wherever he had gone to report us.
After telling them my side of the story, they believed. The officer that sat in the driver's seat told me about his divorce proceedings. And that it was hell. Somehow the Lord would see me through, somehow.
A tow truck pulled up ahead of the cops' car. One of the cops, the older one got out to speak to the driver of the tow truck who walked towards us. They spoke for couple seconds then the cop returned. Then another tow truck pulled up. Doug's car was pulled away. But they were unable to tow Steven's car because he had the emergency brake on. I informed the driver that I could call the owner to unlock the car. I asked to use his cell

phone to call Steven.

"Hi, Steven, you okay?" I was frightened for him. Once again I had put his life in danger.

"Yeah, you?" he asked concerned.

"I'm okay. Listen, the man is about to tow your car but he cannot, because you left the emergency brake on."

"Oh," he must have forgotten.

Steven showed up in less than ten minutes. I wanted to hug him, but I could not. I wanted him to tell me he would not abandon our friendship now, but he said nothing.

He just unlocked the car and then left. The tow truck slowly pulled his car away until it vanished down the street. And once again, here I was standing alone.

CHAPTER 44

SEEKING JUSTICE

Going back to work was the hardest. Facing everyone was the most embarrassing thing I ever had to deal with. Everyone knew. Hours after the incident I had called my supervisor and explained everything to her. She had gone around the office telling everyone out of shock and sympathy. She had advised me to make a report, and I had taken her advice.
That night I went to the 115th precinct in Elmhurst and made a report. That's when I found out that Doug had filed a false report at the 110th precinct in Richmond Hill the morning before he followed me onto the Grand Central Parkway. He'd told them that Steven and I had called the day before and threatened him with a gun. Every organ on my inside quivered. I did not have the strength to go on anymore. Thoughts of suicide filled every vessel in my brain. I did not want to live anymore. It was just too much. This was JUST TOO MUCH!
I knew I had to seek God's strength to carry me through this one. I had not prayed for days, I did not have the zeal to pray now either. But I knew I had to. I remembered when I could fast for days, pray daily. But now it had become more than a task. I had drifted so far behind and did not even know it. Or if I did, I did not care enough to try and make a change. I was going through just too much. It seems as if I just wanted to give up on everything – My Salvation, My Joy, My Life!
Detective D'Ante was put in charge of the case. He could not make an arrest because Doug had filed a report first. How could I let them see that he had lied?
My entire day was ruined. How could I tell Steven that Doug would not be arrested? Could not be arrested? Was this possible? Could anyone do anything and just get away with it? Where was the justice?
I knew then that I would not stop until justice was

served. I knew I would make them see that Doug had lied. They would arrest him! Or I would kill him myself!

The next day Detective D'Ante called me on my job to tell me that he was unable to arrest him because Doug had a different story to tell. For a quick moment I became disoriented. I no longer knew where I was. My head went totally blank. I had to leave work. I couldn't stay. I felt as though I was losing my sanity.
My supervisor was at lunch, but I had to leave. I knew I jeopardized my job by leaving without first informing her, but I just could not stay. Why hadn't they arrested him? I was almost killed. Couldn't they see the holes in his stories? I knew eventually they would, because I would make them believe me somehow.

As I made my way home I just bawled. I didn't cry. I bawled. Life was hell. It was pure HELL! Why me? W-H-Y M-E?!
Sulei's father! The rape. My mother! The abandonment. Doug! Attempted murder. What next?

I then envisioned driving my car over the edge of a bridge. I saw the car stopping and then going over at full speed. I thought of Sulei and Nathaniel. I thought of my funeral. I saw them at the coffin standing over me, crying. Asking why did I do this to them? Why had I left them motherless? But I lay there in the casket I was happy because I would face no more pain, hurt, and disappointments. I saw my mother saying "I'm so sorry. I didn't know." I saw Doug feeling regret for all he had put me through. I saw Sulei's father telling me how sorry he was for taking my innocence the way he took it away that night. I saw it all. Then I saw my face in the coffin. I was at peace. Finally I had peace.

But I couldn't. I wanted to die. I wanted to end it all. But I just couldn't. I was a coward who loved her kids too much. So instead I drove home. The tears came rolling uncontrollably. All I wanted was love. A family and love. Was that asking too much? Was it?

I spent the next day at home trying to fathom a way to make Detective D'Ante see that Doug's story didn't add up. Then that's when it occurred to me. I had gotten Doug arrested before, and I had called the cops on him twice before because of his violent temper. I decided to go to the precincts that had those reports and get copies, then take them to Detective D'Ante.
I called my friend Anthony and asked him to take me to the precincts. I had met Anthony at the Department of Motor Vehicle office when I had gone to get my learner's permit several years ago. We had kept in touch after that. I had invited him to church. He had visited on several occasions. Doug had threatened him too when Anthony had called and Doug had answered the phone. He had threatened to 'punch his face in'. There was no reason for that because Doug and I were no longer together. I had found out that he had gotten a woman pregnant while he vacationed in Jamaica. So there was absolutely no reason for him to threaten anyone. Anthony had just laughed at him. He never really took Doug seriously.

As we drove to the different precincts trying to strengthen my case against Doug, I explained everything to Anthony. He listened keenly without interrupting. Anthony was engaged to his children's mother for the past six years. I never understood why he never took the relationship any further. He always said when the time was right, if the time was right, he would know. Then he would make the right decision. The time never seemed to be right enough for him to take their relationship further. But he seemed contented.

I went to three different precincts, including the one where he had filed the false report. I gathered the evidence needed and returned to the 115th precinct. Detective D'Ante was impressed and saw my determination to prove Doug a liar. He decided to call him in for questioning. Doug was called in to the 115th precinct. He was questioned. Three days later Detective D'Ante called me on my job to let me know he decided to arrest Doug. He decided to arrest him on his job. I was overjoyed. That's all I had wanted. Doug needed psychological help and he needed it desperately. Maybe behind bars he could get the help he deserved. Doug was arrested for attempted vehicular manslaughter.

The Continuation: Surviving

CHAPTER 45

JUSTICE SERVED...

Things got worse after Doug came from jail. He spent three days in jail. At first he was charged with attempted vehicular manslaughter, but then it was reduced to assault. Doug was bitter when he returned from jail. He called Tiffany and threatened her that if she didn't tell me to drop the charges he would tell her husband she was involved in all this. He knew where Tiffany worked and went there after she started refusing to take his calls. He told her many lies about Steven. He told her many lies about my relationship with Steven. He threatened Tiffany that if she didn't tell me to back off, he would go to her husband and to our Pastor.
Eventually he did go to my Pastor. He wanted my Pastor to convince me to drop all the charges. I didn't intend to withdraw *any* of the charges. When all his efforts failed, he went to his son's mother and lied that I had found her social security number and had used her name to get jobs. And worse of all she believed. As much as Doug had abused her physically and had lied to her, and cheated on her, she believed everything he said. He also told her I was illegal in America, and that's why he married me, only to 'help' me.
That's the only truth Doug spoke. I was an illegal alien. He did marry me just to 'help' me.
But what Doug had not known is that while he was in jail I had gone to the Immigration and Naturalization Services (INS) in Manhattan and had gotten approved for my green card. He did not know that I was no longer 'an illegal alien'. I had brought all the papers from his past arrests and the one from his present arrest, and they had approved my case immediately. The officer had told me that once I could prove that he was an abusive spouse I would be granted my green card immediately.
After I was given a card with the stamp of approval I

called my mother to tell her the good news. She had sounded a bit worried. She told me when I reached home to come to see her. Silently I hoped it wasn't Doug again. I just about had enough. Every day I wished to hear that a car, train, or bus killed him. Something. Anything. Just as long as he was dead and never to return. My thoughts were not the best thoughts a Christian should have at that moment, but I really did wish him dead. After getting my green card I had immediately dismissed Doug from my mind. All I could think of was finally being able to visit my grandfather. I had nott seen him for fourteen years. I had not seen my sister, Ilza, for fourteen years either. She had a daughter, Kimberly. I only knew Kimberly from pictures and whenever we spoke on the phone. Now I would get a chance to see them once again. I couldn't wait to see my grandfather and Ilza. I had missed them so much. So very much.

I had just returned from the INS office. The light on my caller ID kept flashing. I realized that my mother had called. I immediately returned her call.
"Hello," she sounded as though she was sleeping.
"Hello, you called?" I asked. I found it rather strange because she knew I was not home. After leaving the INS office I had called to give her the good news of my case being approved. She had said she needed to speak to me when I got home. She knew I could not have reached home so quickly. So I found it strange that she had called my apartment twenty minutes before I reached home.
"Come upstairs, I need to ask you something," there was something strange about her voice. My mother never called me upstairs just to ask me 'something'. She usually does that on the phone.
"Okay, I'll be up." As I placed the phone down, I couldn't help but wonder just what it could have been. I

could not take any more bad news. I was just hanging on to my sanity by a thin thread. I just could not take one more bad news.

As I made my way upstairs, my knees were weakened from anxiety and suspense. My mother's door was opened so I entered. She was sitting at her usual spot at the edge of her bed, leaning against the wall.

"Hello?" I called out but no one answered. "Hello," I repeated louder in a singing voice. I always did that to cheer her up whenever I sensed she was low in spirit. "In here," she managed to say. I could tell she had been crying because her voice quivered. As I entered her bedroom, from the look on her face, I knew right away that my grandfather had died.

He was diagnosed with prostate cancer two years ago. He had gotten worse before, but he always managed to recuperate. But this time he had not. I knew he was ill, but I thought he would have made it at least throughout the year. But he did not. My entire inside collapsed. I had reached my capacity of endurance. My cup had overflowed with trial and pain. I was always strong. At least in front of everyone else I was. I did not shed a tear. Maybe it was pride or maybe I had cried so much already from the pain and hurt I felt from the evil Doug did. But no tears came. Not one.

Chez came over later that night. We both wanted to go to his funeral in Jamaica, but I did not want to take any chance with the temporary evidence of permanence that I received on the card today, not just yet.

I had not seen my grandfather in so many years, and now that I was able to go, he had died. The tears never came when I had stood in my mother's room. But that night as I lay in bed, they came. And they came hard. For the first time I felt released of something that weighed me down. This was my season of sorrow. This was my season of trials.

The days that followed found me depressed and traumatized. I had gone and spoke with my pastor. Our conversation had given me the strength to go on. He did not tell me everything Doug had told him. But he believed everything I said. And to know that he believed in me gave me hope. He believed everything I had told him because I had no reason to lie. And even with a reason, I wouldn't have lied.

Sleeping through the night was difficult. I had nightmares and would sometimes feel as though I lay in turmoil. I couldn't wait to see the morning sun shining through the window. Tiffany and I spoke continuously throughout the days. It was a difficult time for me at work. Every day was another story. Every day I had another story to tell. I was a total mess! Every day I wished to die. I just wanted to put an end to it all. Then that's when I really got to know the purpose of having my children. If they were not in my life, I would have committed suicide. I would have put an end to it all. But my kids saved me. They were the reason I had to live. I had to be strong just for them.
Eventually I prayed. I know the Lord heard my prayer. I allowed my soul to open up. My soul was naked before God. I bawled before the Lord. I N E E D E D him desperately. I was on the verge of suicide and I needed him. No one knew because I remained strong on the outside. But I almost took it all away from my kids. I almost committed suicide because then I thought that was the only answer to all my pain and hurt. That night I cried before the Lord and he comforted me and healed my broken soul.

I wanted to visit Jamaica, but I was still undecided. I

called Ilza and told her of my intentions. She wanted me to come. My grandmother wanted me to come as well. I wanted to go. But I had to make sure I would be able to return before I left the country.

I decided to take the chance to go to Jamaica.

My mother and I left a week later. I used all the money I had to help with my grandfather's funeral. Sulei and Nathaniel stayed with Tiffany. I was regretful that they couldn't go with me to say goodbye to my grandfather. But I did not have enough money for all of us to go.

The week went by quickly. Because no sooner than I had left I returned. I loved my kids. But I must admit there are days when motherhood is just too much! I just wished to be alone on an island basking in the perfect sun's rays, soothed by the fresh air of nature. But the reality of motherhood always rise and hide the rays and tarnish the fresh air of nature when they bickered or did things they weren't suppose to do.

At the funeral I cried my heart out thinking of my grandfather in a coffin. I had taken so many pictures of him as he lay in the casket. I had touched his forehead and was shocked at how hard it was. The image of my grandfather in a box, of my granddaddy in a hole, six feet deep with soil over him never to return stayed with me for a very long time. He was a strong man. But his strength had failed and now he was gone and I would never see him again. I would never hear him tell me, "Mitchy, I love you. You know your granddaddy love you right?"

CHAPTER 46

A NEW PATH!

The District Attorney sent a letter of condolence. I received a temporary order of protection against Doug. Days passed without me hearing anything more about Doug. A deep feeling of fear clutched my inside as I wondered what other plans of evil he had been up to. I prepared myself for anything and everything. I fasted daily and prayed much more. It was the only way I felt comforted. The only way I kept my sanity. As I waited to see Doug's next plan, I left my fate in God's hand and held on tight to my faith.

My mother must have heard the door slammed when I entered the building because she quickly came downstairs. Just then the bell rang. I was startled. I had just come in and hadn't seen anyone behind me. Who could it possibly be?
"Who is it?" my mom asked through the intercom in her usual tone of disgust.
"Detective Johnson," the voice shouted.
My heart fluttered. Why would a detective be at the door?
"Who?" she repeated.
"Detective Johnson, is there a Karlei living here?" he asked.
"Yes, one minute."
As I made my way down the flight of stairs fear controlled my thoughts as I wondered if Doug had been up to his plans again. Or maybe he had died. That's it. The demon had died. Good. I wondered to whom I owed my thanks.
"Yes?" I raised my brows as I cautiously opened the door.
The man at the door was about five feet five inches tall. He had very little hair on his head and a receding

hairline.

"Detective Johnson," he said flashing his badge open.
"Come on in," I said as I glanced downwards to notice the paper envelope in his hand. As I followed behind him I felt *somewhat* relieved.
"What is the problem?" my mother interceded.
I was glad for her interruption and her show of support, because I was at the brink of a collapse. One wrong word to my ear could have caused me to go over the edge.
"No problem, I am here to give Ms. Karlei this subpoena," he said unfolding the letter in the envelope and then handing it to me.
All I had heard was 'no problem'. Nothing else he said mattered. 'No Problem' that was good enough for me. Quickly running my eyes across the paper I then showed it to my mother. It was a subpoena from the Assistant District Attorney's office. Doug was due in court in two days. I thought they had forgotten all about our case because it was almost two months since I last heard from a lady from the Assistant District Attorney office. She had offered me a cell phone in case of an emergency, but I had refused the offer. After all it could only dial 911. The subpoena stated that I had an appointment at the Assistant District Attorney office on Queens Boulevard to state the facts of the case two days before he was scheduled to appear before the Assistant District Attorney. Bitterness immediately crept into my heart. After the Detective left, my mother cautioned me of Doug and told me to do what was right for Nathaniel and me. Then she shared out a serving of ackee and codfish with dumplings, my favorite meal and the national dish of Jamaica.

As I entered the big glass building on Queens Boulevard a demon of fear approached me. But I quickly cast it aside and focused on the Bally's Fitness Club that stood welcoming me through its doors. Ladies with towels loosely wrapped around their necks wandered in and out. I thought, someday when I could afford the luxury I would become a member.

I made my way to the receptionist on the ground level of the building. I opened the letter to see the name of the Assistant District Attorney that I was coming to see. I introduced myself and asked for Mrs. Chambers and went to sit and wait.

The receptionist asked that I sit down and wait for a couple minutes. It seemed like forever until a petite-framed lady stepped towards my direction minutes later. The receptionist was right it did take a couple of minutes. I had doubted her because in the business world, a couple of minutes could turn out to be hours. The petite-framed woman was dressed in a pinstriped navy blue suit. Her shoes were elegant with very high heels causing her to look much taller than she actually was. Her hair was coiled in a bun. Her glasses looked like spectacles back in the 1960's and they balanced on the tip of her nose.

"Hi, I'm Mrs. Chambers and you're?" she trailed off glancing at the paper. But I quickly interjected and completed her sentence.

"Karlei."

"Yes this way please," she said beckoning me to her office.

As I entered her office I sighed heavily. I just wanted to get it over with. I no longer cared whether he stayed in or out of jail. I just wanted to get it over with and move on with my life.

Her office was immaculate apart from the numerous boxes that lined the wall along the window filled with sheets of yellow and white papers. On her desk were two pictures of two children, a boy and a girl. The girl resembled her and had the same dark colored hair as she did, but the boy had blond colored hair with blue eyes. I thought Hollywood would die for those features. I thought maybe they were her kids. Just then I noticed the wedding band on her left hand and a picture on the wall behind her. It was a much larger picture than the ones on her desk. The man in the picture was an exact photocopy of the boy on her desk. That must be her husband and those, her kids.

She asked me several questions about Doug's past and about our marriage. She concluded eventually that what Doug needed was counseling, not jail time, because he would come out worse than when he went in. She said if he was given jail time he would lose his job, which would make him bitter and become a further menace to society. A further menace to society? A further menace to **ME**!!! I totally agreed with her.

So she decided to drop the charges from attempted vehicular manslaughter to assault, which carried a six-month sentence. But she said she would seek for probation and counseling instead. I agreed. I signed the papers and then left.

As I exited her office, I glanced at the clock on the wall above the receptionist's head. The meeting only took forty-seven minutes, but it seemed like two hours. As I exited the building on Queens Boulevard a sudden gush of wind brushed against my face. My life began strolling through my mind and I realized that I did not have anything of importance in my life other than my two children. I wanted more. I wanted more for me, and more for them. I longed to be able to afford vacations every year. I longed to not have to worry about paying an electric bill for $30.00.

I knew one day though I would make it happen, just for them.

The train took forever to come. Then it finally came. I

was glad that there were only two other passengers aboard. As I entered the train my mind wandered to Steven. We had become very best friends since the past month. Steven had matured and began communicating more. He had been in a relationship that had gone sour and caused him to see me in a totally different light. He used to think I was miserable because I inquired of his whereabouts, but now he knew that I had only cared when I questioned him so much.

My thoughts were suddenly interrupted by the ringing of my phone.
"Hello," I said as low as my voice would go as I glanced around to see if the ringing attracted anyone. I hated answering the phone in public.
"Wha'pen?" He asked in his usual happy tone.
"Nothing, I'm on my way home. Everything went okay," I was always happy to hear his voice and to see his face. I had come to realize that I did love Steven and would never stop loving him.
"I have something for you okay," the tone of his voice sparked my curiosity.
"What?" I asked inquisitively.
"I'm not going to tell you," he teased.
"Okay, I'm coming right now okay," I could not wait to see what he had.
He always surprised me. Sometimes it would be something a simple as my favorite dish, ackee and codfish, or something as extravagant as the time he bought me a Gucci bag.
The train seemed to take forever to reach my stop. I walked briskly towards his house from the train station. I rushed up the steps and made my way into his house. The front door of his three floor apartment building was already opened. Slowly walking up the stairs to catch my breath I knocked his door.

He opened the door and grabbed me around my waist and pulled me to him. His kiss was wet and firm. He was the one for me but I was afraid. I was afraid to love him because he was never settled. He hardly stayed home. He was always hanging out with his friends and I already had problems with trust.
Holding my hand in his he placed a small box into its palm.
Pulling away from him I opened it slowly. It was a diamond engagement ring with a wedding band to match. My eyes opened wide in shock.
"Will you marry me?" he asked smiling. "I want you Karlei," he continued, "I want no one else. God believe me! I want NO ONE else but you."
I could not believe it. Steven. I had wanted to hear those words for so long. We had been through SO much together. But I no longer knew what I wanted anymore. I was just so tired. I needed time to think. Furthermore, he wasn't a Christian. But how could I say no? He was all I had ever wanted but was always afraid to fall in love with. I stared blankly at the carpet afraid to look into his eyes. It felt like a dream. I was more afraid to face the reality.
He was all I ever wanted. I knew he was my soul mate. He understood me more than anyone ever did or will.
"I need just a little time, okay?" I couldn't believe after all this time I had wanted him so badly and now here he was giving himself to me and 'I need just a little time *okay*?'
But I did. I needed time. I needed time to think. I needed time to cry my soul away. It was just too real. I needed time to let it saturate within my soul. I needed the time for Steven to be saved first. I couldn't take him as he was. I just couldn't marry another unsaved man!
We hugged and kissed again. That's as far as Steven and I went. We always hugged and kissed. But we never

went beyond that. I was always curious but never took it there. He had asked before, but I always managed to say no. And he respected whatever I said. And I respected him more because of his respect for my feelings. I guess that's why he may have expected me to understand that he had needs and that's why he came home 12 p.m. and 1:00 a.m. But I never understood and never would. Steven took me home. We never spoke though. It was as though what had happened in his apartment never happened. The rings were nice though! But I had to remain focus. But ain't gonna lie, they WERE nice and looked expensive too! I was glad to reach home. My mom had picked up Nathaniel at the baby-sitter and Sulei was home from school. She was eating dinner my mother had cooked when I arrived home. I quickly went upstairs to my mom. Nathaniel was asleep. He was already washed and had eaten also. My mom offered me dinner, but I refused. I didn't feel like eating at all.
I rushed downstairs with Nathaniel. Placed him on my bed and sat beside him. I then opened the box Steven had placed in my hands. The rings were beautiful. I waited a couple seconds before dialing his number.
"Hi," he answered in a romantic voice.
"Hi," I replied smiling at his tone. "Thanks for the rings."
"You're welcome."
We spoke about nothing for ten minutes or so.
As a lay in bed, it still seemed a dream. But I knew it was too real to be anything but real.

CHAPTER 47

A NEW LIGHT

I was glad it was Saturday. Laying in my bed refusing to get up. Just then my bedroom door opened. It was Sulei. She wanted to go to my mom's apartment. She wanted to take Nathaniel with her. I was glad to be left alone.

I decided to invite Steven once more to church but I was afraid he would not accept. So I dialed his number to complete the thought. To my surprise, he agreed to come with us. He said he had thought of giving his life to God for all that he had been through.

I chose not to believe anything he said because I had heard those same words when he had just returned from California. But one thing I knew for sure. I would never marry another unsaved man. I knew I wanted to marry him and spend the rest of my life with him. I would never entangle myself with another man who was not serving God.

I decided to go back to school. I had already completed my General Equivalency Degree [GED] before I had moved out of Doug's house. I then registered at Nassau Community College. I was not sure what I wanted to do just yet so I registered in the Liberal Arts major. It was not easy caring for two kids and going to school. But I had to do what I had to do.

Two weeks later I registered for my first classes at Nassau Community College. I wasn't sure where in life this degree would take me, but I intended to start somewhere.

*****

This all happened almost thirty years ago. Thirty years before knowing that the big apple was down to its core.

My mother and I became very close friends. She sometimes cries and apologizes for all that she had done. But I forgave her many years ago. I knew without all of my struggles I would not be the woman I am today. I love my mother from the bottom of my heart. She is everything to me. Without her I would not have been. My daughter and son would not have been. There is nothing in this life that she could possibly do to me that I could not forgive her of because she has my forgiveness before an act is done or a word is said. Because she is my MOTHER.

CHAPTER 48

A NEW DAY!

Steven started coming to church every Sunday. Three Sundays later, he got baptized. He received the Holy Ghost during one of our Sunday night revival services a month later.

He called me that same night to say how different he felt and what a joy he had missed for so long. He said he felt as though he walked on air. I couldn't believe that finally Steven was saved. Suddenly the tears flowed continuously. I knew then that I *would* be Mrs. Steven. I knew then that I finally had my victory.

I shared the joy with my mother and the entire world. Everyone knew of my ordeal with Steven and the journey we took together. Most called me a fool for not 'getting with him sooner after all he'd done for you'. But after all I've been through I couldn't do it the wrong way again. I wanted it the right way this time.

My mother helped me with the plans for my wedding. It was hectic because of school and work, but we did it. Steven and I saved enough money as a down payment on our first house as our engagement gift. It was not a mansion, but it was everything I had hoped for in a house. It had a roof and rooms and that's all I wanted. When we finally got the keys we took *our* children to see it.

Sulei was ecstatic.

I finally knew how to love and be loved. I knew trials would come, but I was finally contented with my life. I knew with every marriage problems existed. But I was prepared to fight for my marriage. I was prepared to fight to remain a Christian woman and wife.

CHAPTER 49

THE BIG DAY . . .

T he day finally came.

As I entered the church to Mariah Carey's song 'Hero' tears rolled down my face. I worried about the makeup that decorated my face, but was overwhelmed. As I approached him and came closer to him, I realized his eyes were crystallized with water as well.

As my stepfather gave me over to him somewhere inside I always knew he would be mine. But today I was sure. He looked even more handsome in his tuxedo as he stood next to me. I was so proud to be his wife.

As I stood in front of the Pastor and exchanged our vows he whispered in my ears, "You're all I ever wanted and you have nothing to be afraid of. I will love you always Karlei."

The tears rolled even more.

I wanted to stop them from falling. I had pictures to take! But I just couldn't. All my trials. All my pain. They all played over again and again as if in a movie scene.

But I knew this is where they stopped. Right here at the Alter beside Steven. Nathaniel was my ring bearer. Sulei was my maid of honor. As young as she was, she was my maid of honor. No other deserved that title. NO ONE! Chez's daughter, Denise, was my flower girl. Chez was my bridesmaid, and Steven's best friend, Ian, was our best man.

As we said our vows I wondered what my honeymoon would be like. I had always wanted to hold Steven. Really hold him. Not just hold him. **Really** hold him knowing he's mine.

See, there's a certain spiritual connection that's made when two people in love hold each other. It's as though

your spirits leave your bodies and connect as they float upward towards heaven. A certain connection.
My breathing increased by the thought of holding Steven. I suddenly felt dizzy. He must have noticed because he held me closer almost supporting me as I stood next to him. All I remembered of the ceremony was the Pastor asking do I take Steven to be my lawful wedded husband, and I knew I said yes. Then he asked Steven and all I remembered him saying was "heck yes." I couldn't believe he said that in church, but he was a new convert and had a long way to go.

As we made our way through the aisle of our well wishers I saw the faces of all who had bore my pain through the years. Tears overshadowed my mom's eyes as she hugged me close to her breast. And for the first time she told me her how much she loved me and was proud of me. And for the first time I believed. And for the first time I knew she was sorry for what she had done because I saw it in her eyes.

As we continued our way through the crowd there were tears in my aunt's eyes, and in Sulei's godmother's eyes too. Because they knew how far I had struggled to come this far. My mother's friend took her napkin and wiped the tears away from my eyes and whispered that I shouldn't cry anymore. She said the pain was over. The time for joy had come.

As I looked at my husband I knew the joy that was here with us was worth the wait and the pain.

We were showered with grains of rice as we walked towards the limousine that waited for us. My mind wandered to the day this possibility began, the day Steven got baptized. The song that played as he was baptized grew louder in my head.

*"I will rise again
Ain't no power on Earth
Can tie me down
Yes, I'll rise again
Death can't keep me in the ground."*

And as the limousine drove away I knew I had left all my pain in my past. As hard as I tried to not shed a tear, they still kept rolling down. But I knew they were the last drops of tears from my pain from all the years past, to fall. And they fell on my pure white gown. And once again and as usual Steven was there to wipe them away.

And I Will Rise Out of My Valley

CHAPTER 50

LIVING THE LIFE!

I came to America almost three decades ago. My life spiraled out of control. I had a terrible relationship with my mother. Was it that she was a non-caring mother? Or was it that I went through the terrible teen years? It depends on who tells the story.

I went from being raped, bearing a child, homeless, without clothes and food, no job, no green card, abused spouse, low self esteem, and not loving myself.

Today I love me. I love me.
I
Love
Me!
I have found me, like me, love me, and am in love with me.
I have found a woman in me that can make me happy without a man to validate me being a woman.
I have found the one person that never will fail me - God!
I have found the one person that never will deceive me - God!
I have found self-respect and self-esteem. That's important! It's *after* I found those two elements I knew what to expect from people. You cannot know the level of self-respect or love you deserve until you first respect and love yourself.
On the road to finding them though, there will be many 'friends' that you will have to put aside. Why? Because they will be lost to the new you. But that's okay, they're making room for the growth of the new you.
Then, I found a joyful relationship with God. I found God for myself. Now, I have finally found the one man that truly satisfies - Jesus!

It has been a long and hard road. At times I thought suicide. I literally thought suicide. But my kids kept me going. Through the years my mom and I have had many ups and downs. The problem was me. I wanted her to be what I wanted her to be. I had to learn to accept her for who she was. It hurt at times because she is not who I want her to be to me – a mother. But I have found in her a friend. I can call and ask for advice. And she gives me honest and fruitful advice. And that's what she is – a genuine friend. And I had to learn to accept her for who she is and not who I yearned for her to be.
My mom is now a born-again Christian and we have a fruitful and wonderful relationship.

Today, without shame, I can share my story to anyone – a student, a mentee, even a stranger.
My past does not define who I am today. My past is my past. For reasons obvious I do not use Pine Sol to clean, nor do I get attached to anything I cannot walk away from in less than a second. Today, I have found the joy in being Dr. Karlene A. Richardson. I was homeless. I was raped. I was a hustler. I was a statistics.

Today, I am no longer a victim!

Dedicated To . . .

I left the most important chapter for last . . . This book is dedicated to my mother.

She taught me strength. She taught me the true character of being a strong woman.

You may never understand the appreciation I have for my mother – the woman who gave me life. She gave me the gift that allows me to be whatever *I* choose to be. No one chooses who you are but *you*. People may become obstacles and create challenges that prevent you from getting where you ought to be. But no one can choose who you become but *you*.

So how can I *not* forgive when I have experienced the pain of childbirth? How can I not forgive when I too have experienced the toil of the nine-months-period of pregnancy?

The day my mother made the choice to not abort me, and the day she labored in the torment of pain she suffered as she delivered me, she *earned* that forgiveness.

So she is still my mother. She is *still* my mother.

She
is
still
my
mother!

From Gutter to Glory

The closer I get to the prize
The more I plea for humility
For when I see a woman on crack
I say
"There goes I if not for the Grace of God."

For I remember the days
If not for my daughter's face
I could have strayed.

When cast down
Could have been dead
But instead
I rose again
For she depended on my strength within.

And though the strength few,
I hung on to victory
For I rose again
"From Gutter to Glory."

The shackles broke,
The chain, they loosened.
The haters' cries silenced,
For I rose again.

And God said,
"You will not go down like this
For in this world, for you there's a purpose."

And he said,
"You're still my Child
I'm still your God.
You're gonna make it
You're on your way."

And he took me *"From Gutter to Glory."*

You can't forgive without loving.
And I don't mean sentimentality.
I don't mean mush.
I mean having enough courage to stand up and say, 'I forgive. **I'm finished with it.**'

~Maya Angelou

Hi There!
Yes, you!
If you or someone you know has been raped or abuse, do not remain silent. You can get help. Reach out to us at http://nowhealed.webs.com/
Simply fill out the Contact Us form and someone will contact you within hours.
Other resources include:
- Safe Horizon
  (877) 935-7393

- Children's Aid Society
  (212) 949-4800

- Joyful Heart Foundation
  (212) 475-2026

No one should suffer in silence . . .

Join us today in celebrating the lives of women who overcame!

Speak the word ~ **Now H.E.A.L.E.D.!**
http://nowhealed.webs.com/

Made in the USA
Lexington, KY
01 August 2014